the Editor's Companion

Saginaw Chippewa Tribal College
2274 Enterprise Drive
Mt. Pleasant, MI 48858

An Indispensable
Guide to Editing
Books, Magazines,
Online Publications,
and More

the
Editor's
Companion

Steve Dunham

WRITER'S DIGEST
BOOKS

WritersDigest.com
Cincinnati, Ohio

THE EDITOR'S COMPANION. Copyright © 2014 by Steve Dunham. Manufactured in the United States of America. All rights reserved. No part of this book may be reproduced in any form or by any electronic or mechanical means including information storage and retrieval systems without permission in writing from the publisher, except by a reviewer, who may quote brief passages in a review. Published by Writer's Digest Books, an imprint of F+W Media, Inc., 10151 Carver Road, Suite # 200, Blue Ash, OH 45242. (800) 289-0963. First edition.

For more resources for writers, visit www.writersdigest.com.

18 17 16 15 14 5 4 3 2 1

Distributed in Canada by Fraser Direct
100 Armstrong Avenue
Georgetown, Ontario, Canada L7G 5S4
Tel: (905) 877-4411

Distributed in the U.K. and Europe by F&W Media International
Brunel House, Newton Abbot, Devon, TQ12 4PU, England
Tel: (+44) 1626-323200, Fax: (+44) 1626-323319
E-mail: postmaster@davidandcharles.co.uk

Distributed in Australia by Capricorn Link
P.O. Box 704, Windsor, NSW 2756 Australia
Tel: (02) 4577-3555

ISBN-13: 978-1-59963-902-4

Edited by Rachel Randall and Cris Freese
Cover designed by Brianna Scharstein
Interior designed by Michelle Thompson
Production coordinated by Debbie Thomas
Cover images by aleksander1/Fotolia.com

ACKNOWLEDGMENTS

A big thank-you to my editor, agent, and friend, Dave Fessenden, for all his help and his enthusiasm for this book.

A big thank-you also to the people at Writer's Digest Books, who made this book much better than the original manuscript I submitted. Also to all the other people whose expertise I drew on, particularly the late Richard Mitchell, Laura Moyer, the late William Safire, Margaret Palm, Evan Morris, Michael Quinion, and Candi Harrison.

ABOUT THE AUTHOR

Steve Dunham has been writing and editing professionally for more than three decades. He has written for newspapers and magazines, and he has edited journals, books, newsletters, and other media. He has taught short classes in copyediting, publications quality control, and other topics.

Contents

Preface

Editing—who needs it?

As a writer, I need it. I make mistakes. I write things that I think will be clear to everybody, but an editor says, "No, no, Steve," and I realize my error. Thank God for editors. "Nobody loves a copy editor, but everybody needs one," wrote copy editor Laura Moyer,[1] even though we editors "make errors seven days a week," she noted on another occasion.[2]

Editors, writers, everyone—we all make mistakes, no matter how educated we are.

"Many general graduates, though … computer-literate, cannot edit their own résumés," wrote Arthur Plotnik in 1982.[3] It's still true thirty years later. (I saw one résumé on which a man claimed to have been an "adverse weather aerial delivery system." I still have no idea what he was talking about.)

One writer produced an article for an online company publication and didn't think it needed editing, so it got posted as written. A spell-check would have caught the typos—*con-sensus*; *thethreat*; *fo*; *for,and*; *con cluded*; *disaf-fected*; and *dieon*,—but the published article also misquoted a federal law and a federal report, and it cited a symposium that took place "28-18 November 2000." It took an editor to notice that the date was bogus.

If only the U.S. Special Operations Command had gotten an editor involved before circulating a want ad for "technical writters for operational rediness documents."

Editors don't just catch typos, though. We are also responsible for the meaning of the words. The Bureau of Alcohol, Tobacco and

Firearms' reference to its "unique expertise in the use and misuse of fire-arms and explosives" would have benefited from some editing. (I myself have some expertise in the misuse of explosives: On one Fourth of July, I set our yard on fire while shooting off fireworks.)

There's a lot more that editors do—Arthur Plotnik enumerated six skills: "research, strategy, perception, organization, language, and troubleshooting."[4]

This is how I would summarize it: As editors, our task is to assist the writer in the job of communication. Communication might take the form of persuading, informing, convincing, entertaining, or inspiring. *Assisting* the writer might mean rejecting the work if it is being presented to the wrong audience (by submitting it to the wrong publisher) or if it is unsuitable for publication because the writer has not done a proper job.

This aspect of editing—selecting material for publication—is as much an art as a science. It requires taste, sensitivity to the readers' needs and desires, a feel for what is good writing, and a sense of which new and untried material will appeal to readers. Even if you are new to editing, you may find yourself responsible for choosing what gets published, although in some organizations an editor may have no say in those decisions.

Some other aspects of editing are, if not more science than art, at least governed more completely by rules and standards. By standards, I mean Standard English: "the English that with respect to spelling, grammar, pronunciation, and vocabulary is substantially uniform though not devoid of regional differences, that is well established by usage in the formal and informal speech and writing of the educated, and that is widely recognized as acceptable wherever English is spoken and understood,"[5] according to *Merriam-Webster's Collegiate Dictionary*.

Nonetheless, "something may be grammatically perfect rule-wise yet fail the fundamental test of good grammar, which is crystal-clear communication," wrote Rich Adin on his blog, An American Editor.[6]

Editing means not only applying the rules, but also applying good judgment. *Baltimore Sun* copy editor John McIntyre offers this advice:

"If you spend all your time chasing shibboleths and tweaking minor solecisms, you may not take into account that the text itself is vapid and inane."[7] This book is not a substitute for good judgment nor for a style guide, such as *The Associated Press Stylebook and Libel Manual*, nor for a classic work on writing, such as *The Elements of Style*. I could not hope to improve on them or to cover grammar and word usage in such detail or with such authority and accuracy. You will want these and other comprehensive guides on hand to study and reference.

Rather I want to present an approach to editing that answers the questions "What do I need to do?" "How do I do that?" and "Why do I do that?" and helps editors make good judgments.

Not all editors agree on everything, and in some places I've presented more than one viewpoint. Listening to different thoughtful voices is helpful in thinking about writing and editing, and in making our own choices.

I hope that this book will help you learn to apply the rules and standards of written English to others' writing and help writers to better communicate.

Introduction

Do not be satisfied if you write so that someone can decipher
it. Tell your story so that anyone with the right background can
understand and even enjoy it.

—Matt Young, *The Technical Writer's Handbook*[8]

Most of us editors, I think, are editors because we love English. Through
study and work, we've learned what makes writing good, and we've
learned how to bridge the gap between ordinary writing and good writing. We do that by taking writing that has potential and bringing it up to
our standards.

Yes, we have standards. The standards exist because they're proven.
Writers who follow the rules will, on the whole, do a better job of communicating than those who do not. "Language is arbitrary, but it's not
anarchic," wrote the late Richard Mitchell, English professor and the
Underground Grammarian.[9]

There are exceptions. You might arrive at a destination faster by dis-
regarding the traffic laws, but you are more likely to get there every time
if you follow the rules. Writing is like that. You can break the rules and
still get where you're going, but if you repeatedly disregard the rules,
you're more likely to cause a wreck along the way.

In writing there are (perhaps unfortunately) no fines for breaking
the rules. You won't lose your literary license for committing too many
infractions. The only penalty is failure: failure to get your work published, failure to communicate, failure to do the best you can. As writers
or editors, we have our share of failures, but with careful effort we can

enjoy success: getting our work published, communicating with our readers, and doing the best we can.

Not everyone appreciates the value of our efforts. "There are fewer individuals who can recognize good editing from bad [or] no editing, and even fewer who care, being more concerned with cost," wrote Rich Adin on his blog, An American Editor.[10] At the *Baltimore Sun*, "copy editing, in particular, was seen at the corporate level as a cost center, an expensive frill, money wasted on people obsessing with commas," wrote *Sun* copy editor John McIntyre. "… One of the unexamined assumptions of the War on Editing is that readers, comfortable with the lack of editing standards on the Internet, would be fine with low-grade stuff in print."[11]

Is there a war on editing? The "demand for traditional editing skills" is "going away," argued Rufus Griscom of Babble, a parenting website. "… Abundance … is necessary to win online, and it is impossible to produce abundance with intensive editorial process."[12] His blog post, quoted here, had a few errors pointed out by readers, and this, he said, "demonstrated the efficiency of crowd sourced copy editing."[13] So Griscom acknowledged the rules, although not the need to correct errors *before* publication.

"Can't you just fix errors later, after readers notice them?" asks *The Yahoo! Style Guide.*[14]

> Sure, but that's hardly an ideal solution. For one thing, as soon as you publish your story online, you no longer have complete control over it. Someone may copy text from your site—mistakes and all—or take a screenshot of it, or the flawed story may immediately appear in a news feed, which is content that sites export to people who have signed up for it. So, even if you fix an error, your original story could still be out there. And email presents an obvious problem: If you send a faulty email newsletter to thousands or millions of subscribers, you probably can't recover it.
>
> But the potential permanence of errors isn't the only reason to ensure that your copy is posted right the first time. The biggest

reason is this: You want to provide a superior user experience that attracts a loyal audience to your website. People notice mistakes, and seemingly small errors like typos and bad links can make a site look unprofessional or unreliable and can drive visitors away.[15]

■■ Refinement or Seeking Page Views?

Traffic, engagement data, and social media success provide a much clearer picture of the effectiveness of a piece of writing than the opinion of a single editor. Refining one's writing style based on this feedback loop is the best editing process available.

—Rufus Griscom[16]

What Griscom's describing is tailoring your content to produce the most churn. By this standard the best-edited piece in today's Huffington Post is "More Details Surface In Tony Parker Sexting Scandal."

—Bill Barol, *Forbes*[17]

Others besides Barol see the value in editing according to standards and not just in response to a "feedback loop." "Editing is crucial to producing professional communication," says the U.S. Air Force *Tongue and Quill* style guide, which does not hesitate to lay down rules for good communication.

A skilled writer can bend the rules sometimes—and good editors allow that. There are times when sentence fragments convey a message better than complete sentences do. A punchy rhythm communicates certain things: Force. Repetition. Emphasis. And starting a sentence with a conjunction may create continuity rather than disruption.

Other infractions of the rules are hard to get past the language police. Sentences must end with a period, a question mark, or an exclamation point, just as you must stop for every red light. Doing otherwise is too likely to cause harm, and your reader is expecting you to come to a full stop at the end of every sentence. (An unfinished thought might end with ellipsis points; see chapter five.)

The rules work. They help writers get where they want to go—and to take their readers with them. Editors enforce the rules, but we're not just authoritarians, sticklers for obedience, dictators of the language.

"We learn the rules. We apply them," wrote copy editor Laura Moyer. "We're not trying to catalog the language in all its many glories; we're just trying to help writers write and readers read. Punctuation, spelling and grammar are the tools that help make a piece of writing readable."[18]

We editors are here to help writers get their work published, to communicate with their readers, and to do the best they can.

1

Marks of Good Writing

What makes good writing? As editors, we must recognize good writing, because it should be the result of our editing, after we have remedied any deficiencies.

A good writer uses words skillfully, choosing them with care, organizing them for maximum effect.

A good writer doesn't waste words; every word has a purpose and is often chosen over other words that would have served almost as well.

"The way you write reflects the way you think," wrote the late William Safire, the "On Language" columnist of *The New York Times*, "and the way you think is the mark of the kind of person you are."[19]

Good writing presents what the writer has to say. It does so effectively, it communicates clearly, and it makes reading easy for the reader. Consider these words of Walter Lord in *A Night to Remember*.

> "What did you see?" asked a calm voice at the other end.
>
> "Iceberg right ahead," replied Fleet.
>
> "Thank you," acknowledged the voice with curiously detached courtesy. Nothing more was said.

In only four sentences, Lord gave his readers a sense of the command situation on board the *Titanic* on the night of April 14, 1912. A lookout's warning was answered with calm detachment, no questions, no further comments. The writing communicates clearly; the prose provides both information and insight.

Lord's narrative writing makes history easy to digest. His grammar is straightforward, his punctuation orthodox, his vocabulary conventional. The technical terms he uses can be found in a dictionary.

Occasionally he will bend the rules slightly by beginning a sentence, or even a paragraph, with a conjunction: "But most of the crew stuck to the ship."

The writing is concise; it is simple but powerful. It conveys facts plainly, while the drama inherent in the story carries the reader along. In *A Night to Remember*, Walter Lord knew he had a story worth telling; no verbal embellishments were needed to make it interesting. That is good writing.

Not that verbal embellishments are the mark of an uninteresting story. They are one of the writer's tools, to be used when appropriate. Sometimes they are the mark of literature—that is, writing valued as much for its aesthetics as for the information it imparts. Shakespeare's plays are literature. We read *Hamlet* both for its insights concerning human nature and for the beauty of the writing. Some of the dialogue might be improbable, but *Hamlet*'s value is not in realistic speech; rather it is in speech that exquisitely communicates the thoughts and emotions of the characters. Few people in real life might bid a deceased loved one farewell by saying, "Good night, sweet prince,/ And flights of angels sing thee to thy rest." Yet those lines exhibit such poignant emotion that countless writers have chosen to quote them. That is good writing.

Plain writing and fancy writing each have their place; both are tools for communicating. They do not compensate for lack of content; they communicate the content. The writing of Walter Lord and the writing of Shakespeare are both rich in content. Each writer used the appropriate style to communicate with his readers. What writers have to say largely determines how they will communicate it.

Rare is the piece of good writing that has nothing to say. The nonsense poems of Lewis Carroll are one example, but one reason they are humorous is that their sound (poetry) contrasts with their lack of sense. Normally both sound and sense are essential to good writing. "Take care of the sense, and the sounds will take care of themselves," said the Duchess in *Alice's Adventures in Wonderland*, but that is bad advice for writers, because the sounds (the words) do not take care of themselves. Consider, for example, this extract from a May 19, 2011, Homeland Security Department press release: "to prevent, protect, respond to and recover from terrorist attacks, major disasters and other emergencies." The sounds may have pleased someone's ear, but the sense is seriously flawed: Preparedness grants are not designed to "protect … terrorist attacks." Even if we have something eminently sensible to say, our choice of words will not automatically be good. (Even in the mad world of Wonderland, the Duchess's advice was not true: The sounds often made no sense.)

While editors must make sure that the words a writer has put on paper accurately represent the author's intention, an editor also must make sure that a writer really has something worthwhile to say. "The English language … becomes ugly and inaccurate because our thoughts are foolish, but the slovenliness of our language makes it easier for us to have foolish thoughts," wrote George Orwell.[20]

"The editor's first reading of a manuscript is critical of content," says a classic style guide, *Words Into Type*,[21] "appraising its value, detecting its weaknesses and its strong points, judging its literary style and the skill, or lack of it, shown in the assembling of the subject matter." The editor will focus "attention not only on the larger aspects of content and arrangement, but also on details of what the author has written" and how the author "has expressed it."

Content is, after all, the main thing we expect writers to provide. On occasion, when an author has extensive knowledge but little writing ability, a publisher will waive the requirement that a work be well written. A medical doctor or a general, for example, might be a fount of information that deserves to be communicated, yet be only a mediocre writer. In that case, the content compensates for the deficiencies in writing, and an editor or ghostwriter is called to bridge the gap (and sometimes it is a huge chasm) between writer and reader. "Modern English, especially written English, is full of bad habits which spread by imitation and which can be avoided if one is willing to take the necessary trouble," wrote Orwell.[22] Once we take the trouble and bridge the gap, however, the author and editor have achieved only one mark of good writing.

Good Content

Communication, even in writing, requires two people. Every time a writer begins putting words together for publication, one fact should always be foremost: The writing is (at least partly) for the benefit of someone else. Even if a writer begins without a specific audience clearly in mind, the goal of communication remains. The writing must achieve a link between author and reader.

The editor, too, must always remember the reader. Both writer and reader may benefit from written communication, but editing is done primarily to benefit the reader, to smooth the process of communication.

The content of any piece of writing ultimately must be of personal interest to the reader. From news headlines to novels, from apartment leases to the Bible, every piece of writing attracts readers by providing something that concerns individual people.

An editor faces the task of taking a piece of writing and heightening its relevance to those individuals who constitute the publisher's readers or market. This frequently is complicated by the fact that editors may receive very little response from readers.

Focus

Each sentence, says editor Margaret Palm, should convey one idea. So should each paragraph and each chapter, with the ideas becoming more general as the writer progresses up the scale. This sort of cohesion does not limit the number of ideas a writer is able to communicate; rather, it organizes them. Focusing on one idea at a time makes for clear, direct communication. It does not leave the reader guessing where the writing is headed. It does not distract the reader with digression. Instead it takes a general idea as the subject of a chapter, develops an aspect of that idea in each paragraph, and provides details in every sentence. Focused writing, like a focused photograph, presents information clearly.

Margaret Palm compares nonfiction prose to pyramid building. The main idea—defined in a document's title—is like the crowning block atop a pyramid. Below that is another course of stones or ideas, defined by chapter titles in a book or by first-level subheads in an article or essay. Below that are more layers. Actually charting the outline of a piece of writing in pyramid form can help editors to identify the story's organization, including subhead levels, and to spot missing pieces. If, for example, the title or introductory copy identifies three ways to get rich quick (neither writing nor editing will appear in that list), then the editor should expect a chapter or subhead devoted to each method of achieving wealth. If the next course of stones or level of ideas describes the prerequisites, techniques, and time required for each method, then the editor should expect the next level of organization to be divided along those lines.

The typographic heading style for each level needs to be distinctive, and four levels of headings is probably the limit that a typical reader can recognize and keep track of.

The Grinnell College *Scarlet & Black* student newspaper stylebook explained another framework for writing, the upside-down pyramid.

> The classic style of newswriting, with the "most important" facts at the top, followed by less and less important facts in descending order is called the inverted pyramid. Inverted pyramid leads begin with who, what, when, where, why, and how, all in a few sentences.

Those five Ws of journalism also provide a guide for both writers and editors of nonfiction. In a news story, the writer must tell the reader who, what, when, where, and why—preferably in the first paragraph. Although not all nonfiction needs to be as compact as news writing, the editor must be sure that the basic facts are communicated.

Even in fiction, the five Ws need to be addressed somewhere in the story, although depending on the genre—mystery, for example—key parts of the story may be withheld until the end.

Precise Language[23]

Writing is for communication. This is no less true of technical writing than of writing for newspapers, magazines, or books of fiction. Except perhaps for a few novelists or poets, we do not write solely to express ourselves; we write to say what we have to say, so that our audience can understand it.

—Matt Young, *The Technical Writer's Handbook*

The writer's biggest job is that of combining words—and often numbers and graphics—to share ideas. Organizing the material and choosing precisely the right words require more effort than just writing down what is in the writer's head. The knowledgeable writer possesses information or ideas that the reader does not. To make that information accessible, the writer must use words that the reader understands (or explain any that the reader does not). The writer must choose which information to include and must decide what is superfluous or would burden the reader. Appendices, footnotes, and bibliographies are all communication tools. So are abbreviations. They help the reader understand what the writer has to say.

The editor's job is to help the writer communicate with the reader, and just about all of us—including editors—need some help with our writing. Sometimes we have a little trouble saying what we mean. Editors do make sure the commas are in the right place. (It does make a difference: My favorite comma error was in an ad in the church bulletin for a supper hosted by the youth group; it read, "Don't cook Mom!") Editors also do a lot more, ensuring good content, focus, precise language, and good grammar.

Editors are on guard for much more than missing commas, however. Writers might, for example, get a little repetitive: "The analysis phase of the project consisted of analysis," stated one report I read. A job ad required "program related experience in related areas"—one of those "necessary conditions that must be met."

"Better say nothing at all. Language is worth a thousand pounds a word!" as Lewis Carroll wrote in *Through the Looking-Glass.*

The reader's time is worth something, too. Let's not waste it by stating the obvious. If our work is read voluntarily, we will lose readers if we waste their time. Often, though, we may be editing a piece of writing that people are obligated to read, and we owe it to them to communicate simply and clearly.

In *The Island of Doctor Moreau* by H.G. Wells, the Monkey-man— a monkey that Doctor Moreau had been trying to turn into a human—"was for ever jabbering ... the most arrant nonsense" and "had a fantastic trick of coining new words. He had an idea ... that to gabble about names that meant nothing was the proper use of speech. He called it 'Big Thinks' ... He thought nothing of what was plain and comprehensible."

Writers can commit Big Thinks by using imprecise language or misusing words entirely. Some writers may impress themselves by using big words they don't understand. *Utilize* may sound more impressive than *use* (but has a specific meaning of its own: to find a use for). *Comprise* is not the same as *compose* (it means "be made up of," as in "New York City comprises five boroughs"); a *nation-state* isn't merely a sovereign country (it's the country of a single nationality); *coalesce* isn't transitive (things coalesce, people don't coalesce things). *Emulate* means "do at least as well as," but *imitate*, the word that is more likely appropriate, doesn't sound nearly as impressive. *Respective* is often used where it is not needed, as in "The adjutant generals report to their respective governors"—well, of course they report to their *own* governors. Writing to impress oneself or others is what editor Dave Fessenden called "the curse of Babel." He pointed out that people built the Tower of Babel to make a name for themselves and ended up with their language confounded—a result still obtained by vain and pompous writers, he said.

Editors must be alert to misused words. *Words Into Type* has an excellent twenty-three-page list of "Words Likely to Be Misused or Confused"; *The Elements of Style* has a similar list, and *Merriam-Webster's Collegiate Dictionary* has usage notes for many entries. (See also chapter seven.)

In his book *Doublespeak*,[24] William Lutz described another way of misusing big words: "gobbledygook or bureaucratese ... a matter of piling on words, of overwhelming the audience" or "inflated language that is designed to make the ordinary seem extraordinary." That language is meant to impress, and specifically to deceive, the reader.

Aside from writers who deceive themselves, readers are usually the victims of misused words. As William Safire wrote in his book *In Love with Norma Loquendi*,[25] "Meanings can be assigned to words to suit the speaker, corrupting communication and derailing intelligent discourse."

For example, one job description stated, "Demonstrates technical achievement at the highest Government and corporate levels." In plain English, what does that mean? It sounds as if the job applicant must have been president, chief justice, or speaker of the house. Such overblown prose corrupts communication and derails intelligent discourse, to borrow Safire's wording.

When writing and editing, let our first concern be the reader. Let's not try to impress anyone, least of all ourselves. Instead of engaging in Big Thinks, let's pursue the goal of "plain and comprehensible" communication.

Another thing to keep in mind is that we tend to write for people who like to read. We like to use literary references, subtle distinctions, and humorous allusions. It's easy for writers to forget that some people *don't* like to read. For some, reading is a chore (perhaps because poor writing has made it so). Our job as writers or editors often requires us to communicate with those people, too—and with people who don't have time to read everything we want to say. Sometimes a message needs to fit onto a bumper sticker.

In his book *Spread the Word*,[26] William Safire quoted President Clinton's remarks on how to summarize his administration's social policy.

> "We were trying to think of what our bumper sticker would be," said the President at a luncheon, seeking to change the Administration line from "less shock, more therapy" ... "I think our slogan would be there needs to be more reform and more social service support," Mr. Clinton said, "more attempts to build a safety net to deal with the consequences of reform, but not an attempt to slow down the reform effort."
>
> Some slogan.

As Safire's sarcasm emphasizes, clear communication often falls victim to wordiness and complexity. When a slogan is called for, a whole paragraph is ruled out. As journalist Edwin Newman wrote, "What we ought to be demanding is that our leaders speak better English, so that we know what they are talking about and, incidentally, so that *they* do."[27]

As communicators, we may need to pass on information that affects everyone in a company, and those people may need that information in writing. That calls for clarity and simplicity. The compound sentence may be out of place. The nuance and metaphor may be distractions. In such cases we need simple statements, questions, and commands.

Forms are a good example. Bulletins and announcements are others. The questions they ask and the information they convey need to be clear and unmistakable.

At ANSER, a company where she and I worked, an artist, Elaine Sapp, was asked to create signs that read, "Effective Feb. 1, 2000 ANSER employees will no longer be able to park in the designated spaces." Forty of the signs were going to be posted in the garage.

Elaine came to me and said, "This isn't right." She knew that we could do a better job of communicating the intended message. When she was done with them, the signs read, "No ANSER Parking." (The original wording was also a good example of why commas are needed before and after the year: *2000* could be read not only as a year but as a number of employees. "I wonder how I'll know if I'm one of the 2000 employees that can't park here," commented editor Dave Fessenden.)

From time to time I've attended children's church services. I've noticed that when the pastor simplifies the sermon to make it understandable for children, the adults seem to follow it better, too. To communicate in a simple way doesn't have to mean leaving anything out. It means presenting the important points in order. It means stating exceptions clearly. It means not assuming too much prior knowledge on the part of the reader. It means presenting conclusions plainly, based on the information already presented. These are good rules for all writing that is meant to provide information.

Good Grammar[28]

"I don't care about grammar," a writer told me when he brought his article in for editing.

In fact it seemed that the writer, like many others, didn't care about a lot of things.

"This merger does not seems to posse any intimate security risks to the United States" was one statement in the article. I called out the posse of language deputies; we changed *posse* to *pose* and fixed dozens more errors, grammar and otherwise. We had to query the author to find out what *intimate* was supposed to be (he'd meant to use *immediate*).

Unfortunately this writer was not alone. Not in making mistakes—we all make those—but in not caring. George Orwell cited two common faults in English writing: "staleness of imagery" and "lack of precision. The writer either has a meaning and cannot express it, or he inadvertently says something else, or he is almost indifferent as to whether his words mean anything or not."[29]

If a writer doesn't care about grammar, the writer at least should care about the reader. If you have something worth saying, then care about communicating it.

The editor, who is assisting communication between writer and reader, must scrutinize every piece of writing that is intended for publication and, to the greatest extent possible, make the text conform to the marks of good writing.

Author Stephen Coonts, in a July 2001 interview with *Proceedings of the U.S. Naval Institute*,[30] discussed the editing of his books (the Naval Institute Press published his first novel, *Flight of the Intruder*).

Proceedings: How were you treated, editorially, at the Naval Institute Press, compared to your subsequent publishers?

Coonts: The Naval Institute is unique, because it probably publishes more first-time writers—not so much first-time novelists, but first-time writers—than any other publishing house I know. So for me it was a great place to learn how to write by working with the editors and to learn how to get a manuscript up to what is called "commercial quality."

Subsequently, I went to Doubleday, where they have a line editor who looks at the manuscript and puts in some commas and takes some out. How you wrote it is the way it's going to be in the book. It's tough for most beginning writers to get their prose ready to be published. It was a really great educational experience at the Naval Institute. I worked with a great editor, and I learned a lot.

Proceedings: So you'd say you were edited more at the Naval Institute Press?

Coonts: Yes. They edited the living hell out of the book. I think they overedited some of the passages. In some cases they improved it; in some cases they made it worse. Looking back, I don't think they had much faith that I knew what the story I was telling was all about. On the other hand, the folks I worked with knew their English, and what a sentence was, and how the prose had to come together. On balance, it was a great learning experience for me.

As Coonts pointed out, editors make mistakes, too. Sometimes we attempt to improve clarity and end up muddying the water instead. Worse, we sometimes accidentally change the correct meaning to something incorrect. "One of my greatest dreads as a copy editor is that I will change something to make it wrong," wrote copy editor Laura Moyer in her Red Pen blog.[31] "Changing things on the proof is risky, as it raises the possibility of introducing an error while attempting to correct an existing one," she wrote in another blog entry.[32] Editing for focus, precision, and grammar are essential and less hazardous than editing for content, which requires some knowledge of the subject matter.

Furthermore, overconfidence can lead to wrongly second-guessing an author's meaning. An editing error in *Under Two Flags: The American Navy in the Civil War* by William M. Fowler, Jr.,[33] led to a cure that was worse than whatever the supposed illness was: "*Galena* was far smaller than *New Ironsides*, 738 tons versus 3,486; her topsail schooner rig and exaggerated tumble made her home immediately recognizable." When I read that, I suspected that it should have read, "… her exaggerated tumblehome made her immediately recognizable"—*tumblehome* being the inward curving of a ship's sides as they rise (some ships, anyway). *Galena* indeed was immediately recognizable because of her exaggerated tumblehome (see the photo). Evidently the nautical term *tumblehome* was unknown to the editor, who rearranged the sentence into immediately recognizable words (the author confirmed that this was an editing error but added, "Alas, I read proofs").*

An extreme example of second-guessing the meaning was a reference to a story in the *Atlanta Constitution* headlined "Mock Bioterror Attack Spooks Some in Denver." Someone citing it decided it was a mistake and, in a footnote, changed it to read, "Mock Bioterror Attack Some Spooks in Denver."

Both the word *tumblehome* and the *Atlanta Constitution* headline were verifiable with a little research. Second-guessing the meaning (rather than looking it up to verify it) is one hazard for editors.

---

* That is, he saw proof copies of the pages before publication but didn't notice the error.

USS *Galena* (1862–1872, showing the exaggerated tumblehome);
U.S. Naval Historical Center photograph.

Arthur Plotnik, author of *The Elements of Editing*, noted another:
Editors "must stop short of a self-styled purism and allow for some variety of expression."[34] All editing requires care to ensure that the writing communicates better than it did in its original form.

Plotnik posed ten questions for editors to critically examine their own work:[35] Has the editor

1. "weighed every phrase and sentence … to determine whether the author's meaning" was preserved?
2. "measured every revision … against the advantages of the author's original"?
3. "pondered the effectiveness of every phrase"?
4. "studied every possible area of numerical, factual, or judgmental error"?
5. searched "for typos and transpositions, especially in" parts that were "retyped or reorganized," and "edited and proofread" the portions altered by the editor?

6. "groveled in the details of the footnotes, tables, and appendices"?
7. "cast a legal eye upon every quoted phrase, defamatory comment, trade name, allegation, and attribution"?
8. "stepped back to consider the impact of the whole as well as the parts"?
9. "provided all the editorial embellishments to the text—title, subtitle, subhead, author notes, sidebars …"?
10. "cleared every significant revision and addition with the author?"—if that "is the policy of the publication."

As Plotnik's list indicates, editors must be certain that they are actually improving the author's writing. Overconfidence comes all too easily, and we need to handle the author's creation with care.

2

Editing for Content

Editors of magazines, books, and online publications are continually searching for the right content. Every publisher is serving a particular market (often competing with other publishers for the same market) and must repeatedly provide new content to the readers in that market.

"Editors have historically had two jobs: finding interesting material, and making it better," wrote Rufus Griscom of the parenting website Babble. "Next generation editors, if we still call them editors, will do two things: identify great content creators, and help them package and distribute their content in a way that is mutually beneficial."[36]

Each market comprises readers with shared interests. A publisher of books or magazines about sports must produce a continuous stream of new material about sports. Every sport has its passionate adherents— baseball fans have a voracious appetite for more information about baseball, for example. The publisher reaching that market can sell baseball books to fans year after year, as long as the publisher's writers can provide strong new content. The publisher can even sell some football books to baseball fans, because a fair proportion of baseball fans will be football fans, too. The same publisher would waste time and money producing a book about quilting, however strong the content might be, because only a small number of the sports fans in the publisher's audience would also be interested in quilts.

According to author Stephen Coonts:[37]

> The big thing every would-be writer has to understand is that publishing is a for-profit business. The publishers have to make

a profit, or they won't want to do your next book. And the novelist has to deliver a product that the publisher can, indeed, sell for a profit. …

Understanding that publishing is a for-profit business is a hard lesson for most authors to understand. They do one book, and they think they can write anything they want for the second. The answer to that is no. You got there with one book that fits into a genre, and that's where the publisher wants you to stay. That's where the money is. If you go outside that genre, you're going to take a huge financial bath. The public that bought your first book may not want your next one. What you find out is that publishing is a business, and so is writing.

Some publishers are not-for-profit, but they still have to operate in the black. Being nonprofit means that the business does not exist to benefit the owners or officers but rather to serve some public good. The publications might indeed be subsidized by some other source of income, but not-for-profit does not mean that, overall, the organization operates at a loss.

This discussion of publishers as businesses brings up an important point: Publishers must care about the needs and wants of their audience. As an editor of content for a publisher, you need to care, too.

Writing for the Reader

What is appropriate content for any given publishing house depends on its readers—primarily the existing market, such as magazine subscribers or the people on a book catalog mailing list, but also the readers a publisher hopes to add to its market. The publisher of baseball books, for example, might plan a series of publications about classic stadiums and introduce that series to possible new customers for that publisher: readers interested in architecture.

Present the Information the Reader Wants

This would bring into play another consideration: What content does each market want? While a book on baseball stadiums would probably be of interest to both the baseball and the architectural markets, the publisher must consider the differing desires of the readers. The readers whose primary interest is baseball might want to know more about the structure from the players' point of view and might also want a list of every baseball team, including visiting teams, that ever played in the stadium. The readers whose main interest is architecture (there will be some baseball fans among them) will want to know about alterations to a stadium since its original construction but also might enjoy a list of the teams that have called the stadium home. The right content depends on the desires of the readers.

Many books fall short in the supplemental material they provide: photos, maps, appendices, tables, and so on. If there are photos, they should illustrate the major elements, particularly those things that are hard to visualize from a verbal description alone. If there are maps, they should show the places mentioned in the text and their relationship to one another. Appendices can provide more detail about topics mentioned in a book, or they can provide the complete text of documents that are excerpted in the main part of the book.

One of the editor's tasks is to identify the things in the text that need to be amplified elsewhere.

Know Your Readers—Their Sensitivities, Sensibilities, Knowledgeability, and Reading Level

"Know your audience," wrote Candi Harrison in her Candi On Content blog. "This is where you start. This is the first step, and you can't skip it. Who are you trying to serve? Who is your audience?

"Don't forget about those unanticipated customers," she continued, "—the ones who show up and without an invitation."[38]

Harrison was referring to readers who visit a website, but the principle applies to almost any book, magazine, or other publication. Will someone who casually comes across your publication become a regular customer? That's partly up to the author and editor: Have they crafted the content for an unnecessarily narrow readership?

The editor must consider not only the appropriate level of detail for every given topic, but also the reading ability of the people buying the publication, as well as their tastes. If quotes from baseball players include profanity, should those remarks be quoted? It depends in large part on the sensibilities of the readers: The editor "will see to it that the sensibilities of the readers … have been respected and not unnecessarily offended," states *Words Into Type*.[39]

Conversely, "a portion of what editors have done in the past—removing bias, encouraging a measured consistent tone—makes writing less engaging to most readers," asserted Rufus Griscom of Babble.[40]

However, "to appeal to the readers' interest does not mean to salute their every prejudice," wrote Arthur Plotnik.[41] Indeed some publications have always emphasized colorful, even lurid, material over more sober writing.

Rarely, though, will an obscene remark aid the work of communication (although it could reflect something important about the character of the person being quoted). *The Associated Press Stylebook and Libel Manual*, under "obscenities, profanities, vulgarities," states: "Do not use them in stories unless they are part of direct quotations and there is a compelling reason for them."[42]

Another source of offense is arrogance. One book manuscript that came to me concluded: "This book was birthed from the heart of God! It was inspired by the Holy Spirit. Read and obey." Even supposing it were true, getting readers to pay for and listen to your message might be easier if you exhibit some humility rather than give orders.

Editors must judge carefully in other cases, too. Many readers do not want to see God's name used loosely, and a good editor will exercise discretion when choosing to include, omit, or edit such things.

To return briefly to Walter Lord: A good many oaths and curses probably were uttered on the night the *Titanic* sank, but few of them appear in *A Night to Remember*. One salient blasphemy appropriately does appear, however: A crew member told one of the passengers, "God himself could not sink this ship," and Walter Lord not only quoted him, but used those words as the title of a chapter.

A neutral use of mild profanity might be unavoidable (and generally inoffensive) within a context—in baseball, for example, a reference to the musical *Damn Yankees.*

It is worth noting that profanities and obscenities not only have lost some of their shock value from overuse, but rarely were "strong language" to begin with, although they often have been called that. "Strong language is not strong at all but weak, reflective of stupidity," wrote Robert D. Smith.

> … it is reflective of brutalized persons who wish very much that they knew how to speak forcefully. … Christ used strong language. He identified the Pharisees, to their faces, as a "brood of serpents" (Matt. 23:33), and as "like whitewashed tombs, beautiful to look at on the outside but inside full of filth and dead men's bones" (Matt. 23:27).[43]

Judith Martin ("Miss Manners") offered another view.[44]

> When people who don't want to look prissy argue against the promiscuous use of profanity, they always state the case as follows: … constant use of those standard curse words demonstrates a poverty of language skills.
>
> All that swearing is terrible because it just goes to show that people don't know how to express themselves forcefully.
>
> This implies that if only the swearers would make more of an effort, they could think of all kinds of vivid and imaginative ways to insult the world and offend everyone in it.

Truly strong language that communicates clearly *without* needlessly offending is often in short supply where it is most required, and editors appreciate authors who can communicate strong sentiments without resorting to either clichés or profanity.

Nor should the fact that profanities and obscenities have become commonplace on television lead editors to assume that such words will sit comfortably with their readers. A careful editor will not use television as a guide to acceptable language.

Writing is like taking your reader on a canoe trip down a river, Ed Harding, editor of New Wine Press, told me. The reader will fetch up on the rocks every time, he said. That is, every obstacle to communication— not only inappropriate profanity, but such things as an ambiguous sentence, incorrect punctuation, wrong word choice, or an extraneous argument—constitutes a rock in the river, waiting to rip the bottom out of the reader's canoe. One of the editor's tasks is to remove the rocks and so help writer and reader to complete their journey uninterrupted.

Not that editors should force writers to compromise what they have to say—good writing is sometimes harsh, challenging, or controversial. Rather the editor's job is to ensure that the writer keeps the work focused and does not distract the reader from the message.

Make Reading Easy for the Reader

A writer's use of English, whether good or poor, makes an impression on the reader—a bigger impression than the writer may realize. Even when the reader may not know correct usage from incorrect, the quality of the writing will be evident just by how well it communicates.

It is better for a writer to communicate well than to impress the readers with a large vocabulary. While editors should not shy away from making sure the author uses the most precise word for any situation, neither should editors encourage the use of obscure words or jargon.

"Too often, complicated and jargon-filled documents have resulted in frustration, lawsuits, and a lack of trust between citizens and their government," according to the Plain Language Action Network in *Writing User-Friendly Documents*.[45]

Jargon often gets used without thought, leading to runaway metaphors and convoluted conundrums. Here are a few real examples.

networks that can tie the aeronautical arena together

sustained, dramatic growth, which continues to be a catalyst for growth

Can an arena be tied together? Can growth be a catalyst for growth? "A string of words can just as easily express inanities as ideas," wrote Richard Mitchell.[46] Readers shouldn't have to wonder whether the author has something sensible to say. Editors need to cut out any inanities and help the ideas shine through, identifying the meaning (often by interacting with the author) and eliminating the defects of expression that H.G. Wells described:

"You puzzle over the thing for a long time and end with the suspicion that not only do you not understand it but that the author does not understand it either," wrote H.G. Wells in *The Food of the Gods*, referring to scientific papers. "But really you know many of these scientific people understand the meaning of their own papers quite well: it is simply a defect of expression that raises the obstacle between us."

Sometimes the obstacle may be not just a difficulty in communicating a complex idea, but needless use of technical terms that may be well understood by the author but not the reader.

"People are easily confused by the unfamiliar, good enough reason for sticking to plain English the rest of the time," wrote Michael Quinion on his World Wide Words blog.[47]

If you use "unnecessary jargon, or specialized or technical terms," then "some of your visitors won't understand what you're saying," advises *The Yahoo! Style Guide*. "Even those who do may have to slow down to get your exact meaning."[48]

Writing for the Web—where much published writing appears— means you might have an international readership. To accommodate foreign readers, an editor should watch for unnecessary use of dialect, local references, and words that mean different things in other countries (for example, a biscuit in Britain is a cookie in America). Writing for that international readership "also makes a translator's job easier, if you offer your content in multiple languages," notes *The Yahoo! Style Guide*. However, "making your content understandable to people with varying reading skills doesn't mean dumbing it down or losing your unique voice. Be literal, simple, and clear, and use your best judgment about what will sound natural to your audience."[49]

"Use words, phrases, and descriptions that your customers use and understand," wrote Candi Harrison. "Speak their language—don't make them learn yours."[50]

Also think about how people will find your publication if it is on the Web. Content may not be easily searchable because "the words on the page are not words that the searching audiences use or recognize or—in many cases—even understand. ... if people are searching using terms that don't appear on your web page, they probably won't find that page," wrote Harrison.[51]

"Our language sometimes goes through painful phases, usually at the hands of small groups of people who inflict it with their jargon, the gibberish of the moment, the emerging dialect of a profession or social movement," wrote Paul G. Hayes, a staff writer for the *Milwaukee Journal*. "... Every profession has its jargon. ... It is when the insider's jargon gets outside that the language suffers. ..."[52] The answer is to put jargon in its place.[53]

Jargon has a bad name. In fact it is, by definition, bad: "confused unintelligible language," says definition 1a in *Merriam-Webster's Collegiate Dictionary*, 10th edition. Definition 1b is no more encouraging: "a strange, outlandish, or barbarous language or dialect." The dictionary provides three more definitions: (1c) a hybrid language, (2) technical terminology, and (3) obscure and often pretentious language.

The Associated Press Stylebook and Libel Manual gives only one definition: "the special vocabulary and idioms of a particular class or occupational group." I think that misuse of those special vocabularies has earned jargon its reputation as unintelligible, barbarous, or pretentious.

"Most of our unnecessary jargon consists of words like 'interface' and 'input,' precise namings at one level of technology, which seep downward into lower levels where they are neither precise nor even needed," wrote Richard Mitchell.[54]

Jargon, like any other vocabulary, should aid communication. "Every field has its jargon, its specialized terms and phrases," wrote John

Holdren of the Core Knowledge Foundation in his article "What Are We Thinking? What Are We Saying?"[55]

"Lawyers have their writs, torts, and depositions. Doctors speak not of cuts or scrapes but lesions. Computer specialists banter about baud rates, RAM, and downloading.

"In the legal, medical, and other scientific fields, such jargon is usually employed for the sake of technical accuracy."[56] In such cases, jargon helps people communicate with one another. That is the place for jargon.

"Every craft has its technical lexicon, and the terms often make useful and necessary distinctions between one thing and all other things, sometimes exceedingly fine distinctions," wrote Richard Mitchell. "The more technically demanding the craft, the more it needs an extensive and precise, technical lexicon."[57]

Holdren, however, questioned the overuse of jargon by educators, especially in their communication with people outside their profession.

> Many parents say that they sometimes find the jargon of education mystifying and intimidating ... I have to agree with them. Unlike scientific and legal jargon, [in] educational jargon ... many of the words refer to no concrete thing or specific action. Some terms— such as "holistic" or "process-based" or "mastery learning"—have little more apparent substance than the dust that blows from erasers clapped together at the end of a school day. ...
>
> Whenever we say or hear a term that only we as educators are likely to use ... it should trip a little mental tape loop that asks, "Why am I using this word or term?"[58]

Educational jargon, wrote Richard Mitchell (who was a college professor), is "a kind of vocabulary of special terms, each of which is used to conceal an emptiness of meaning and to make the obvious sound important. ... A term that means almost anything means almost nothing. Such a term is a convenient device for those who have almost nothing to say."[59]

Is the jargon we use—whether in the context of science, law, medicine, computers, education, or another area—helping us communicate? Or is it sending a different message?

Jargon, said Holdren, can be "a kind of verbal secret handshake that says, 'No outsiders allowed.' This is especially worrisome when the outsiders are those whom we need to be our allies." Not only education, but most fields have some kind of outside constituency. Businesses have customers. Scientists depend on their funding sources and sometimes on public sentiment as well. Government has an accountability to the voters. The military services depend on public support not only for their budgets, but also to enlist new members.

When writing for our own group, it is easy to assume that our jargon will be understood. However, with so much being published via the Web, we should ask whether outsiders will understand our jargon—especially ordinary people who turn to our websites to learn from what we have to say. Those outsiders should be welcomed with plain, clear writing.

With this in mind, the advice of *The Associated Press Stylebook* is appropriate: "In general, avoid jargon. When it is appropriate in a special context, include an explanation of any words likely to be unfamiliar to most readers."

Above all, use jargon only to communicate. "If we use jargon to exclude, to obscure, or to mystify," wrote Holdren, "then eliminating jargon from our speech is more than a matter of aesthetic fine-tuning: it is a moral imperative."

A good rule to follow in editing is to eliminate words that don't appear in a dictionary, unless the publisher is certain that every potential reader will know their meaning.[60] A reader who doesn't know a word should at least have the opportunity to look it up. If it is necessary to use unusual words, particularly words that can't be found in an unabridged dictionary, then the words should be defined at their first appearance. Provide occasional reminders of their meaning later so that the reader is not burdened with memorizing new words and their definitions.

Another problem is "common words used with new or rarely used meanings," said editor Dave Fessenden. "One favorite of academics is using 'inform' not with the common meaning of 'to tell (someone)' but with the rare transitive verb form meaning 'to give character to,' as in 'My reading informs my writing.' Many academics seem to use 'inform' incorrectly, as a synonym for 'enhance.'"

Such a rule is no substitute for editorial judgment, however, because new words are continually entering currency, and the editor must decide whether the readers will know their meaning or whether the words should be defined.

In her memoir *Behind the Scenes*, Elizabeth Keckley recorded an exchange between Senator Charles Sumner and President Abraham Lincoln concerning the verb *tote*, "defined in our standard dictionaries as a colloquial word of the Southern States," said Sumner. "… I should prefer a better word; but since it has been established by usage, I cannot refuse to recognize it."

Tote went on to become standard, but it can be hard to know which new words, even if they make it into dictionaries, will enjoy long usage and which will soon fade.

Michael Quinion, besides hosting the World Wide Words blog, also watches for new words that might deserve to be added to the *Collins English Dictionary*. "Some of the additions" (for example, "*BGT*, which sounds like a sandwich but is an abbreviation of the title of a popular TV show, *Britain's Got Talent*," and *tweetheart*) in 2010 were "heavily biased towards evanescent words from the online world, television and politics," he noted.[61]

Editors, therefore, have to decide whether a new word will communicate better than an existing word and, if it will communicate better, guess as to its likely longevity. Having a house style (see chapter five) eliminates the need to make the same decisions over and over, although decisions about word usage sometimes must be made separately for publications intended for different audiences.

In technical or historical works, or other writing that contains specialized language, a glossary can be a helpful addition to the text.

In religious works that quote extensively from centuries-old versions of the Bible (the 1610 Douay Version and 1611 King James Version being the two oldest English versions still in frequent use), some writers have a tendency to lapse into seventeenth-century English themselves. While certain readers prefer the older versions of the Bible, there is no need for modern authors to write in archaic English.

Plain Language[62]

Good Writing Is Good for Business

"How you communicate—the words you use and the ways you organize them—brands your organization as much as that little logo you use or those razzle dazzle graphics or those expensive ad campaigns," wrote Candi Harrison in her Candi On Content blog. "That's why getting the words right—making them 'plain'—is good business."[63]

■■ Writing Clearly

"'Plain' means *information you can find, understand, and use quickly and easily*," wrote Candi Harrison. "So, in addition to choosing the right words, how the information is organized and presented is critical to making content 'plain.'"[64]

Here I want to present some advice from people who have considered how to write clearly: the Plain Language Action and Information Network and the author George Orwell. Their lists don't apply to every piece of writing or editing, but the principles are worth reflecting on.

WRITING READER-FRIENDLY DOCUMENTS
The Plain Language Action and Information Network produced a catalog of writing sins and their corresponding virtues in *Writing Reader-Friendly Documents*. The forty-five-page manual is a compendium of basic writing

principles—principles often ignored, especially in technical and government writing.

- "Identify your audience."
- "Organize to meet your reader's needs."
- "Use a question-and-answer format."
- "Use 'you' and other pronouns to speak directly to readers."
- "Use the active voice."
- "Use the appropriate tone."
- "Write clearly."

"How can you write more clearly?" the authors ask.

- "Use short sentences."
- "Write to one person, not to a group."
- "Use the simplest tense you can."
- "Use 'must' to convey requirements."
- "Place words carefully."

The document also suggests ways to reduce ambiguity.

- "Keep subjects and objects close to their verbs."
- "Put conditionals such as 'only' or 'always' and other modifiers next to the words they modify. Write 'you are required to provide only the following,' not 'you are only required to provide the following.'"
- "Put long conditions after the main clause. Write 'complete form 9-123 if you own more than 50 acres and cultivate grapes,' not 'if you own more than 50 acres and cultivate grapes, complete form 9-123.'"

The authors also advise writers to "avoid words and constructions that cause confusion."

- "Undefined or overused abbreviations and acronyms."
- "Two different terms used for the same thing (car, vehicle, auto, conveyance—choose one)."

- "Giving an obscure technical or legal meaning to a word commonly understood to mean something different (defining 'car' to include trucks)."
- "Strings of nouns forming complex constructions (surface water quality protection procedures)."
- "Pronouns that don't clearly refer to specific nouns."

"How can you make your documents visually appealing?" the authors ask.

- "Use lots of informative headings."
- "Write short sections."
- "Include only one issue in each designated paragraph."
- "Use vertical lists."

Writing Reader-Friendly Documents can guide writers toward clarity. It's good. It's free. Download it. Use it. Share it.[65]

A SELF-EXAMINATION FOR WRITERS
George Orwell presented a self-examination for writers.[66]

A scrupulous writer, in every sentence that he writes, will ask himself at least four questions, thus:

1. What am I trying to say?
2. What words will express it?
3. What image or idiom will make it clearer?
4. Is this image fresh enough to have an effect?

And he will probably ask himself two more:

1. Could I put it more shortly?
2. Have I said anything that is avoidably ugly?

Marketability

The question of marketability always is on the publisher's mind. Generally readers must desire the product enough to buy it, and the willing buyers must be reached at a reasonable cost. In some cases no purchase is involved; even those publications that are free, however, must attract readers.

From the editor's point of view, a work's marketability is achieved by keeping in mind the prospective audience and tailoring the work to those people. This presumes that the writer, the publisher, or perhaps an agent has identified a prospective audience for the work in question—a vital, though sometimes overlooked, part of publications planning.

The Right Structure and Length for Your Market

> The White Rabbit put on his spectacles. "Where shall I begin, please your Majesty?" he asked. "Begin at the beginning," the King said, very gravely, "and go on until you come to the end: then stop."

This passage from *Alice's Adventures in Wonderland* contains good advice for writers and editors. There are, however, occasions when it is proper to begin somewhere other than at the beginning.

The First Salute: A View of the American Revolution by Barbara Tuchman[67] begins with the title incident: the first time the flag of the united colonies was saluted by a foreign power. Then the narrative turns to the events leading up to that salute.

A writer or editor sometimes places the most exciting incident in a narrative—particularly in a first-person, personal-experience story—up front to engage the reader's sympathy and attention, then backs up through time to the actual beginning of the story. In this situation, or with any flashback, it is essential to clearly identify shifts in time. If a story begins at the climax, then jumps back in time, the use of the past perfect tense throughout the remainder of the book will be burdensome for the reader and difficult for the writer to sustain. It may be clearer to use some kind of break in the text to identify the time shift—a dateline or a statement, such as "Twenty years earlier ..." In that case, however, it is important to let the reader know whether this shift in time is a temporary flashback or a permanent change, with the rest of the story following in chronological order. The editor, however, should always question whether a shift in time really is necessary.

No matter where the story begins, it is important to give the reader enough information at the beginning to know what is going on. A writer should not, for example, introduce so many characters or names (even in nonfiction) that the reader has trouble remembering who they are.

"Go on until you come to the end: then stop," as the King told the White Rabbit. That's good advice, but a modern reality makes some people, such as Rufus Griscom, disagree: "The length of an article or post has become relatively unimportant. Space [online] is free, and it really doesn't matter whether or not readers finish articles."[68]

Editor and former newspaperman Dave Fessenden has this to say: "An article online can be as long as necessary, but it probably should be written something like an inverted triangle news story, with the most important information first and the progressively less important details following."

Always, the editor must keep in mind not only what the author is trying to convey but whether the reader is getting all the information necessary to receive the communication.

The Right Level of Detail for Your Market

Many writers make the mistake of including too many details that are not germane to the story. In nonfiction this may mean a surfeit of background information, peripheral details, or dates of minor significance. A book I really wanted to enjoy was *The Trail of the Blue Comet*.[69] The *Blue Comet* was a Jersey Central train between Jersey City and Atlantic City. I rode Jersey Central trains many times when I was younger, and I traveled over parts of the route followed by that underdog passenger train, the *Blue Comet*. Unfortunately the book goes into too much detail: who owned which company, which bonds were sold to whom on which date, and other minutiae. Hardly any schedule change seems to go unremarked. I wanted to read about the *Blue Comet*, the lines over which it traveled, the towns it served, and the history of the Central Railroad of

New Jersey. I did not want to read about the details of nineteenth-century financial transactions, and the extra baggage almost kept me from finishing the book. In technical writing or academic research, such detail may be necessary, but the editor should consider whether it belongs within the narrative or in an appendix.

A book or article is just as likely to suffer from the opposite fault: not providing the level of detail that the reader wants. This may be due to laziness or the writer's inability to see things from the reader's point of view. For example, *The Passion of Jesus and Its Hidden Meaning*, by Rev. James Groenings,[70] is marred by an abundance of surmise—things that "undoubtedly" or "probably" happened, as well as things that are stated to have occurred but for which no evidence is presented. In *Queen Mary* by James Steele,[71] little is said about the ship's voyages, except for the final one, after which the ship was retired. Both of those books left me disappointed.

The perceptive editor must watch for things that are missing and, when necessary, ask the author to conduct further research or interviews.

The Right Material for Your Market

This is probably the hardest puzzle for writers and editors to solve. From time to time I've been on panel discussions with other editors, and writers have often asked, "What do editors want to see?"

An answer I've heard a few times, and it's a good one, is "Something I'd never thought of." Publishers are continually creating and amending their plans for new books and future articles. Generally they know where to turn for authors, and they are more likely to choose experienced authors who have met their needs before—those who not only produce good writing on the chosen subject, but do so on time.

Editors and publishers are delighted, however, to receive a proposal for an excellent book or article. Many times, as an editor, I have assigned writers to interview people or research a topic. And many other times, to my happiness, I have received articles with fresh ideas and subject matter that never before had entered my mind—and with pleasure I published the articles, to the joy of the authors and, I hope, the readers.

Choosing material for publication is something of an art. Publishers tend to stick to two somewhat safe choices: "more of the same" and "the same but different." They also choose brilliant new writing and sometimes radically different writing. But not one of those four choices is guaranteed to sell.

The right material for the market is elusive, and publishers rely on instinct and experience to select the writing they will publish. Whichever writing they choose, it is never made more marketable by being unfocused or poorly written, so editing for content leads into copy editing: addressing the details of composition to turn writing into good writing.

■ 3 ■

Editing for Focus

The best writing reflects the author's ideas and communicates them clearly to the reader. Yet "all communication is, at best, an approximation of meaning," wrote Michael A. Bailin, president of the Edna McConnell Clark Foundation.[72] Part of the editor's job is to keep the writing close to its intended meaning. This task extends from the beginning to the end of every editing assignment.

Beginning With a Strong Opening

The first words of any piece of writing reveal its focus (or lack of it). The writer has many opportunities to engage the readers or lose their interest, but none so crucial as the opening words. Those words give the readers an idea of how the piece is written, the tone of the writing, what the author has to say, and why the readers should care.

The writer and the editor must carefully consider the readers' needs and desires throughout any piece of writing, but especially at the beginning. As mentioned previously, the introduction of too many names—whether in fiction or nonfiction—and the use of technical terms or unfamiliar proper names can burden the reader so much as to make reading a chore. Even in technical writing, the editor should have, as one goal, clear and easy communication. Therefore, the construction of the opening of any story requires careful selection of the material to be introduced first.

The Opening Gets the Reader's Attention

> This guide has been prepared for direct dissemination to the general public and is based on the most reliable hazard awareness and emergency education information available at the time of publication, including advances in scientific knowledge, more accurate technical language, and the latest physical research on what happens in disasters.[73]

Can you tell what this guide is about? That fifty-word sentence certainly gives you an idea of how the piece is written. But what does the author have to say, and why should you care? That sentence is the beginning of *Are You Ready? An In-depth Guide to Citizen Preparedness*, published by the Federal Emergency Management Agency. It is "designed to help" citizens "learn how to protect themselves and their families against all types of hazards." It doesn't really answer the question the title poses—whether you are ready—rather it is more a guide to help you find out. But the opening sentence doesn't tell you what to expect from the guide; it sounds more like a description of the guide for the benefit of workers at the agency. It also doesn't help that it's written in the passive voice.

Lest you think I'm going to pick on government publications, here's the opening of another government document, and it succeeds at its mission.

> The events of October through December 2003 on the night shift of Tier 1 at Abu Ghraib prison were acts of brutality and purposeless sadism.[74]

The independent panel reviewing the abuses at Abu Ghraib prison in Iraq got the five Ws—who, what, where, when, and why—into the first sentence and didn't pull any punches. The opening gives a clear idea of what's going on and what is to come.

The Opening Sets the Tone

> It was the best of times, it was the worst of times, it was the age of
> wisdom, it was the age of foolishness, it was the epoch of belief, it
> was the epoch of incredulity, it was the season of Light, it was the
> season of Darkness, it was the spring of hope, it was the winter of
> despair, we had everything before us, we had nothing before us,
> we were all going direct to Heaven, we were all going direct the
> other way—in short, the period was so far like the present period,
> that some of its noisiest authorities insisted on its being received,
> for good or for evil, in the superlative degree of comparison only.

Who am I to quibble with Dickens? Skip to the next section if you like.
I thought it worth quoting the whole eighty-four-word sentence that
opens *A Tale of Two Cities* because even though the first two clauses
are familiar, you have to reach the end of the sentence to find out that
he wasn't necessarily agreeing with the "noisiest authorities." Yet the
tumultuous events of the French Revolution described in the book do
merit a few superlatives, and the sentence gives you an idea of the kind
of writing that will follow, although it gives no hint of what the story
is about.

Here's another opening.

> Carmen's romance with Broderick had thus far been like a train
> ride, not the kind that slowly leaves the station, builds momentum,
> and then races across the countryside at breathtaking speed, but
> rather the one that spends all day moving freight cars around at
> the local steel mill.

It's not really a beginning at all, or rather it's a beginning and nothing more. It won a "dishonorable mention" in the 2008 Bulwer-Lytton
Fiction Contest (Western Division) "to parody bad opening lines of
novels."[75] It's witty, and you get a clear idea of what the rest of the story
would be like, if it existed.

The Opening Introduces the Story to the Reader

> In the beginning God created the heaven and the earth. And the earth was without form, and void; and darkness was upon the face of the deep. And the Spirit of God moved upon the face of the waters.

***

> Call me Ishmael. Some years ago—never mind how long precisely—having little or no money in my purse, and nothing particular to interest me on shore, I thought I would sail about a little and see the watery part of the world.

In each of these two beginnings, the first few words are familiar to countless people. The opening words of the King James Version of the Bible certainly go to the very beginning as far as religion is concerned. And the next few words immediately develop the creation narrative: God made a formless earth that awaited a divine hand to shape it.

Herman Melville's famous words "Call me Ishmael" allude to the Bible: Ishmael was the son of Abraham and Hagar, and he was banished to the wilderness. The opening three words of *Moby-Dick* are mysterious, though: They suggest that Ishmael is a pseudonym for the narrator, wandering in the wilderness. Then the second sentence shifts quickly to an almost carefree style, scarcely hinting at the ordeals ahead.

The beginnings of the Bible and *Moby-Dick* each lead into a long book that follows directly from the first few words and, at last, resolves itself in a way that is clearly tied to the beginning. The Bible opens with the beginning of the world and closes with the end of the world. *Moby-Dick* opens as Ishmael begins his journey into the wilderness, and it closes with him alone in the wilderness, about to be plucked from it.

Sticking to One Subject

As discussed in the previous chapter, a common obstacle to communication is the omission of important material or the inclusion of extraneous material. Focusing on the subject can be difficult, though: "To go on, mind, hand, pen always restricted to writing upon one single subject, and speaking through the mouths of a few characters, was intolerable drudgery" for Cide Hamete, the fictional author of *Don Quixote*, so in Part 1 he "availed himself of the device" of tales within the novel "which stand, as it were, apart from the story," wrote Miguel de Cervantes. In the "Second Part he thought it best not to insert" such additional stories, "either separate or interwoven, but only episodes, something like them, arising out of the circumstances the facts present … and as he confines and restricts himself to the narrow limits of the narrative … he requests … that credit be given him, not alone for what he writes, but for what he has refrained from writing."[76]

Writers, while they have the microphone, so to speak, can be tempted to inject their thoughts on unrelated topics or burden the reader with information that is not germane to the subject. Instead of limiting their creation to a solid pyramid of ideas, they add a Sphinx over to the side, a couple of temples up the river, and maybe an oasis off in the desert. In this very book, I myself discovered some clever, charming parts that didn't really fit, and I deleted them before other editors could tell me, "No, no, Steve."

Our nonfiction must be timely, interesting, and factual. It shouldn't be filled with the author's opinions unless it's an essay. The facts should convey the message, letting the reader draw conclusions from the facts. If it's necessary to explain the implications of the facts, then the explanation should be supported with quotes from others, if possible.

In fiction, the story should convey the message (if there is one), allowing the reader to draw conclusions. As with nonfiction, it shouldn't be filled with the author's opinions. A well-written story helps the reader see the point of view of the main characters, understand their problems, and identify with their feelings. It's a virtual walk in somebody else's shoes, and if it instills understanding or inspires compassion, enough said. The writer doesn't need to state, "And the moral of the story is …"

So how does the editor find and remove unneeded explanations or opinions? Editor Dave Fessenden says that frequently he starts to remove something but later finds that it is a crucial point—it was just introduced too soon. He suggests breaking down a major piece into chapters and sections, identifying what the theme or focus needs to be, and then removing anything that doesn't help present that theme. This reflects a principle I was taught by EEI (formerly known as Editorial Experts Inc.): Read the whole piece of writing before you start to edit it. Get a perspective on its structure, its main points, and its flaws. Don't just start hacking at it. I've committed this fault many times; when I see a flaw in a piece of writing, I mentally start sharpening my little hatchet and start carving the work into shape before reading it all.

Closing the Circle

Whether we're editing a short news piece or a large book, we need to make sure the ending relates to what has gone before and *completes* the piece of writing. In technical writing, a document often closes with a summary, restating all the main points. In a mystery, the ending may provide some final answer. In literature, the ending might be some final insight or even a question. The style of the ending should be appropriate to the genre of writing, but the crucial aspect of the ending is that it follows from everything that has gone before. (The exception would be the short news piece: If written in inverted pyramid style, it's constructed so that it can be ended almost anywhere for the sake of length, because each paragraph is less important than the one before it.)

Initial evaluation of the manuscript might reveal that the ending is perfect, or it might indicate that the ending is inadequate. The editing work itself might suggest another ending if the ending needs to be changed.

The essential concern of the editor is to make sure that the ending is fitting and will close the story for the reader.

■■ 4 ■■

Editing for Precise Language

Luckily for those of us who wish to be known as writers, there are people … who are content to perform feats of editorial sleight-of-hand behind the scenes and who, should it occur to a writer to thank them, would pretend that their ingenious "save's" were but the usual tidying up of grammatical loose ends. If I am a writer today, it is because my betters tugged and teased and bullied and seduced me into learning a craft, when all I had to begin with, like so many hundreds of others, was a talent. So I did learn; I go on learning.[77]

—Brendan Gill of the *New Yorker* staff

If editors tug, tease, bully, and seduce writers, it is because they see what writers are trying to do and want to assist them in reaching the goal. A writer with talent, such as Brendan Gill (and countless others), has something to say and a pleasing way of communicating it. But even the most able writers make mistakes. A writer who has abundant talent may still produce a convoluted sentence, presume too much knowledge on the reader's part, use the wrong word, or give an incorrect citation.

The editor must be able to see the writer's goal* and then make the writing conform to the task of communication. When the writer's message is clear to the editor but less than clear on paper, this is where we have the opportunity to make those ingenious saves.

The editor may save the writer from looking foolish if the writing contains a statement that sounds all right at first but on closer examination turns out to be absurd; may recognize an allusion and supply the proper citation, saving the writer from unintended plagiarism; and will frequently see that a writer's idea could be better communicated by choosing a more precise word.

The Right Words

> Common usage is not good usage when it loses a useful distinction.
>
> —William Safire[78]

Words are our tools in trade. They are our medium of communication. They form a bridge of thought between the writer's mind and the reader's. To find the right word, therefore, is sometimes to find a treasure. The right word can supply a meaning that no other word can provide. It can lift writing from ambiguity into lucidity. The editor, therefore, never should be content to let poorly chosen words remain. An editor who assists a writer in the task of communication by supplying the right word is like someone providing directions to a traveler: With a little help, the traveler will arrive at the destination sooner and more surely.

"Editing must be done word by word, sentence by sentence, paragraph by paragraph," wrote *Baltimore Sun* copy editor John McIntyre. As an editor you have "to identify the flaws in a text so that you can pick it up out of the gutter, brush it off, clean it up, shave it, and make it

---

* "When editing a book, I almost always find myself referring back to the proposal," says editor Dave Fessenden. "It often presents the writer's goal better than the manuscript does! We have even asked authors to give us a proposal even though we have already accepted the book, because the proposal may describe a book that is different from the manuscript."

respectable"—pick "up a piece of prose and [know] when you are finished with it that you have made it better—more accurate, more precise, clearer, more effective."[79]

Ambiguous Words and Phrasing

One important editorial task is to eliminate ambiguity. If something can be read two ways, some readers will read it the wrong way. Take, for example, the newspaper headline "Police Shoot Man With Knife."[80]

One way for editors to catch ambiguities is to make a game out of catching them. Try to read things the wrong way. It not only can turn dry reading into something enjoyable, it trains the mind in the habit of spotting ambiguities.

What was this Justice Department press release trying to say? "President George W. Bush Granted Pardons."[81] It sounds like the president *received* pardons, particularly because headlines are normally written in the present tense, so readers who are used to that could expect that *granted* is passive voice rather than past tense. The late John Wohlfarth, a writer and editor, suggested "President George W. Bush Issues Pardons." That makes it clear, though I would not have included his first name and middle initial. People would have known which President Bush I meant.

Another source of ambiguity is the casual use of shortcut expressions such as *and/or*. "How easy it is for an editor to fall into the colloquial trap," wrote Rich Adin on his blog, An American Editor. "… we have become inured to constructions such as and/or and too often skip over them, assuming that any reader will fully understand what is meant because we think we understand." The problem, he noted, "isn't that and/or isn't sometimes correct; rather, it has become a way for an author to fudge. … it covers all the possibilities—which is exactly the problem: the possibilities aren't being narrowed."[82]

Editor Dave Fessenden has this to say on the subject: "Writers sometimes try to gloss over a very complex relationship by using and/or as an abbreviation, when the better thing might be to give an example of when one point is true, and contrast it with an example of when the other point is true, as well as when both points are true. And/or may cover all the possibilities rather than narrowing them down, but it can also truncate the possibilities, making a relationship seem simpler than it really is."

Another source of ambiguity lies in what William Safire called "Janus words" (named for the two-faced god in Roman mythology)—words with contradictory meanings.

> Janus words retain both the original and the changed senses. … If words exist to communicate meaning, Janus words are not good words. They communicate confusion. … Consider *showstopper*, "spectacular performance that causes the audience to interrupt with applause" … Can it be that this new word—barely seventy years old—has developed an opposing sense? Apparently so … "something that presents an insurmountable obstacle" [quoting Professor Richard Gambino of the State University of New York at Stony Brook] … Clarity lovers, awake! Stop this Janus word before it splits the lexicographical screen.[83]

One answer that may serve: *deal-breaker* as a substitute for a bad *showstopper*.

Other Janus words are *survivable* and *actionable*. *Survivable* means "nonfatal," something a person could survive, such as a highway crash that results in no fatal injuries. Yet some writers, especially in the military, have been using it to mean "able to survive," such as a "survivable" drone. *Actionable*, for many years, only meant something inviting legal action, something you could be sued over. It has acquired another meaning: something that can be acted on to your benefit, such as "actionable information." Editors need to watch out for Janus words and either replace them with something unambiguous or make sure that the intended meaning is clear in the particular context.

Evan Morris, the Word Detective (on his website,[84] in his newspaper column, and in his book, all called "The Word Detective") has good discussions of many contradictory words—or apparently contradictory words, such as *flammable* and *inflammable*, which both mean "easily ignited" (sometimes the prefix *in-* means "not," but with *inflammable* it refers to something being "in flames").

A problem related to ambiguity is that of phrases that convey a meaning literally opposite to what the author intended. The literal meaning of "All that glitters is not gold" is "If it glitters, it's not gold," which is the opposite of the intended meaning. Unfortunately this hackneyed cliché has been mimicked countless times with a bad effect on grammar and a confusing effect on readers—and listeners. Here's another maxim: "Not all proverbs exhibit good grammar."

I heard the awkward but erroneous "not all" construction while riding with one of my sons on a train. The conductor announced, "Please exit only where you see a member of the crew. All doors will not be open." My son immediately spotted the contradiction and asked rhetorically how anyone would get off the train.

Consider the literal meaning of the following sentences, none of which is true: "All editors are not unfriendly"; "All proverbs are not true"; "All that is written is not publishable."

Now here are three similar-sounding but true statements in clear English: "Not all editors are unfriendly"; "Not all proverbs are true"; "Not all that is written is publishable."

Is either of the following statements true? "All broccoli is not poisonous"; "Not all broccoli is poisonous."

Before you protest that "All that glisters is not gold" comes from Shakespeare (*The Merchant of Venice*, act II, scene vii, line 65), keep in mind that not every Shakespearean idiom is an appropriate pattern for modern communication; also, look at what Thomas Gray wrote in "Ode on a Distant Prospect of Eton College."

> Not all that tempts your wand'ring eyes
> And heedless hearts, is lawful prize;
> Nor all, that glisters, gold.

Notice that, even though Gray had three commas too many, at least by modern standards, he did keep "Not all" and "Nor all" together.

Primary and Secondary Definitions

I've learned to stop and look up a word whenever I'm in doubt. Even better, sometimes I stop and look up a word when I'm not in doubt, and sometimes I turn out to be wrong. Besides Janus words with their opposite meanings, some words have different and sometimes unrelated meanings. For lively, humorous discussions of words and how they got their meanings, take a look at *The Word Detective* book and website. If you want to know what being an unmarried man has to do with getting a bachelor's degree, Evan Morris, the Word Detective, has the answer. In English, "we often use the same word (or what appears to be the same word) to mean wildly different things," he wrote. "In many cases, all the senses of the word do spring from the same root, and all the meanings are at least remotely related. In other cases, however, two words with entirely different histories have ended up being spelled (and often pronounced) in exactly the same way"—for example, "English actually has four separate 'bounds,' each with its own history."[85] He also noted that "'homographs,' words spelled the same way but with different meanings, often derived from different sources and unrelated in their development, are not uncommon in English"; he gave the example of *jet*, which is really two words, one referring to a spouting or throwing, and the other referring to a kind of coal.[86]

Denotations and Connotations

Beyond their dictionary definitions, words often obtain further associated meanings, or connotations, through use. *Clever* means "skillfully inventive" but is sometimes used patronizingly to suggest that someone is adaptive but not terribly intelligent. *Relationship* sometimes has a very minimal meaning—today a "relationship" might be shallow, wrote William Safire: "no commitment, no hurting, just touch lives and run."[87]

The level of formality affects the tone as well. It's easy to notice the difference in documents, such as business proposals, that were written by more than one author. One career summary of an employee will refer to Jack Jones or Sue Smith by their first names while another will refer to Mr. Jones and Dr. Smith. Using first names suggests companionable co-workers; using surnames with honorifics suggests sober professionals. Either might be appropriate, depending on the inclinations of the people awarding the contract. (And "the use of 'Mrs.' is appropriate whenever a woman prefers it," wrote John Geddes, managing editor of *The New York Times*.[88])

The tone of the writing can have other purposes, too, as pointed out by Richard Mitchell, the Underground Grammarian: "No meaning is added to 'Your rent is overdue' when the landlord writes, 'You are hereby notified that your rent is overdue.' What *is* added is the tone of official legality, and the presumption that one of the rulers is addressing one of the ruled."[89]

Merriam-Webster's Collegiate Dictionary says that honorifics are used with one's social superiors. *The New York Times* uses them with everybody, even criminals, making the newspaper look ridiculous rather than overly polite when it referred to, for example, "Mr. Bin Laden."

I think the Associated Press style is sensible—refer to people by last name unless further identification is important, and don't call people "doctor" without specifying the degree unless the person is a medical doctor or dentist, because that's what most readers take "doctor" to mean. And don't add "Dr." in front of a name that is followed by a degree; that would be redundant.

Careful Word Choice[90]

The careful writer thinks about the meaning of each word and looks for the best choice to communicate an idea. Although dictionaries will help identify the best word, often we need to think about the implications of a word or phrase, or just think about the way it sounds.

For example, another editor asked me, "Should we leave 'the foreseeable future' in a document?" Ordinarily I would aim to delete the phrase "the foreseeable future," because often the context suggests just the opposite, indicating that the authors are not sure what will happen in the supposedly foreseeable future. However, astronomy is one subject in which the future really is, if not foreseeable, at least predictable with a high degree of accuracy. (In its helpful list of misused words and expressions, *The Elements of Style* calls "the foreseeable future" a fuzzy cliché.)

You will find conflicting rules for the use of some words. The nice distinction is (or maybe used to be) that *entitled* refers to publications or rights and *titled* refers to nobility. However, *Merriam-Webster's Collegiate Dictionary*, 10th edition, says *titled* can be used for publications and nobility, and the Associated Press says not to use *entitled* for publications, only for rights (as in entitled to a trial by jury). So the use of these words could go any way except in using *entitled* for nobility.

Sometimes I will change something just because I don't like the way it sounds. I realize that this may be vanity, yet I hope that in a few decades of editing I have developed a sense for what sounds good, whether or not it is technically correct. For example, I don't like the sound of *input* when it refers to comments or opinions from people. I like *feedback* even less, as it reminds me of screeching microphones. I would prefer to receive a response, a reply, an answer, an opinion, or comments rather than feedback.

"I always smile when I read about 'a drug deal that went bad,'" wrote copy editor Laura Moyer—"Because, you know, there are so many good ones."[91]

Here's an example of thinking about the way words sound: *Or* means "one or the other" or "one or both." I would use it differently according to context. In the phrase "authored or co-authored" it would sound funny to me to say "authored and co-authored," as though the writer did both for every paper. Adding *either* would help: "She either authored or co-authored." To use a different example, "It rained or snowed forty days this year" suggests to me that it did one or the other or both on forty days; since both on the same day is a possibility, adding *either* would be incorrect. "It rained and snowed forty days this year" sounds as if it did both on every one of forty days. "There have been eight tropical storms and hurricanes this year" sounds okay to me, though, and I don't think it implies that there were eight hurricanes, just that there was a combination of eight tropical storms and hurricanes.

Another thing to watch for is local references. Will they be understood by readers outside the area? Although *The Washington Post* and other papers in the Washington, D.C., area often refer to "the District" (meaning the District of Columbia), in other parts of the country some other district is more prominent, and the word *District* by itself in a headline means, for example, a school district. Unexplained references to the Mall in Washington, D.C., may puzzle readers outside the area, who may not know that it means the National Mall, the park surrounded by monuments and museums and major government buildings, and not some shopping center.

The Right Voice

Some years ago at a writers conference, the keynote speaker—an editor—was urging his audience to use the active voice rather than the passive. As an example of the passive voice, he gave this sentence: "Jesus was sad." Even editors can make fools of themselves publicly.*

In the active voice, the subject of the sentence does something;† in the passive voice, something happens to the subject. It's easy to remember, because the grammatical meaning is paralleled in everyday speech: An active person does things; a passive person lets things happen.

"Jesus was sad" is in the active voice. *Was* is the past tense of the verb *is*. The sentence is an example of a predicate adjective (that is, the object of the verb is an adjective—*sad*—that describes the subject). Conversely, "He was corrected" is in the passive voice. Something happened to the subject.

"It will be phased out by the end of 2006" is in the passive voice. Microsoft Word's grammar checker suggested changing it to "The end of 2006 will phase it out."

---

* I wasn't the editor in this story. I *have* made a fool of myself publicly, but this wasn't one of those occasions.

† "This is true," says Dave Fessenden, "but overusing 'to be'" (*is* and *was* are forms of the verb *to be*) "is as mind-numbing as passive voice, because it's static; there is no real action. The subject doesn't 'do' anything; the subject just 'is.'"

Generally, the active voice is preferable. "At the heart of every good sentence is a strong, precise verb; the converse is true as well—at the core of most confusing, awkward, or wordy sentences lies a weak verb," states *The Writer's Handbook* of the Writing Center at the University of Wisconsin–Madison. "Try to use the active voice whenever possible."[92]

Why? The active voice provides "directness and vigor," says *Words Into Type*.[93] Passive voice tends to make the action anonymous. "Although the passive voice has legitimate uses, it is a weak voice ..." states *Words Into Type*. "Its main function in narration is when the acting agent is unimportant or obvious: for example, 'the suspect was arrested.'"[94]

"In the active voice, people actually do or say things," wrote E.J. Dionne, Jr., in his column "Chattering Class" in *The Washington Post Magazine*.[95] "They're responsible for their behavior. In the passive voice, things just sort of happen; nobody in particular has any specific role in making them happen. The passive voice is sometimes necessary—as in cases when you can't determine who did what—but often it's a great evasion."

Consider the information conveyed by "Steve was poisoned by eating broccoli" versus "Marlene poisoned Steve by feeding him broccoli."

As Dionne suggested, sometimes a writer will make the action intentionally anonymous. In his July 4, 1861, statement to Congress on the suspension of habeas corpus, Abraham Lincoln deliberately used passive voice. "In the drafting of that document," wrote William Safire, "the President's wish to distance himself from that decision is evident: he went through it all [in the last draft] changing the active voice to passive. 'I decided' became the bureaucratic 'it was decided'; 'In my opinion I violated no law' was changed to 'It was not believed that any law was violated' ..."[96]

An author, therefore, may have reasons for keeping action anonymous.

Passive voice, however, can also be a cover-up for inadequate research. Expressions such as "It is believed ..." or "It was reported ..." or "I was told ..." ask the reader to accept a statement on greater authority than the writer's own. Therefore, a writer should identify sources in some way (even if the source can't be named because information was given on condition of anonymity).

I am always on guard when an author states that something is "common knowledge" or "well documented" but gives no documentation. Many things that are common knowledge are not true; it is common knowledge, for instance, that Nero fiddled while Rome burned.

The Right Tense

Most narrative writing is done in the past tense, simply because most events we write about are already in the past by the time we get them on paper. The present tense can convey a sense of immediacy, and some authors have successfully written stories in the present tense.

Here's an example of a few sentences in the present tense.

> I'm coasting downhill at fifty miles per hour, and there's a tractor-trailer right behind me. Suddenly a school bus coming up the hill turns on its flashing lights. Do I hit the brakes? Is the truck behind me fully loaded? Will it be able to stop?

In most cases, though, the present tense is not the natural form of expression and is hard to sustain, and writers tend to lapse into the past tense, which is the natural tense for writing about things that have already happened. In addition, when you write nonfiction in the present tense, the facts may change before your writing is read, a danger that is particularly present when quoting people. A good rule is to put all attribution in the past tense, because people can and do change their opinions. "'I eat all the ice cream I can get,' said Dunham" is safer than "'I eat all the ice cream I can get,' says Dunham." Before your writing appears in print, Dunham might find broccoli ice cream for dessert and retract his statement.

Keep the Chronology Straight

An editor must take care to see that the tenses in any piece of writing are consistent. At any point in a story, any reference to an event further in the past or yet to occur must be clearly identified by use of the proper tense.

This excerpt from *Pierced by a Sword* by Bud Macfarlane, Jr., is a good illustration of muddled tenses.

> Sunday Evening
> 8 October
> The sky over Mishawaka, Indiana
>
> Denny prepared to land the Cessna. He was one of that rare breed—the natural born pilot. Dennis "Denny" Wheat, twenty-four, gently touched his Cessna 172 down on the homemade airstrip on six acres of land within walking distance of his parent's farmhouse. …
>
> He had been obsessed with flying since he saw a documentary about the Wright Brothers on television at the tender age of five.
>
> Even then, Denny knew that he would spend as much of his life as he could sitting in a pilot's seat.

Everything is properly in the past tense until we learn that "he had been obsessed with flying," which is properly in the past perfect tense. Immediately the narrative reverts to past tense. Is he, at age twenty-four, planning to fly as much as possible, or did he, at age five, make that decision, as suggested by the context but not the tense? The paragraphs that follow switch back and forth between past tense and past perfect tense but don't clearly correspond to the time periods being discussed. Changing "Even then, Denny knew" to "Even then, Denny had known" would make it clear that at the age of five he wanted to be a pilot.

Then there was the curious case of Richard Corfield, in which his teenage years apparently occurred before he was twelve: "I was 12 when *Pioneer 11* departed the Jupiter system. During the bulk of my teenage years, *Pioneer 11* had been arcing high above the plane of the ecliptic."[97] Because his teenage years came later, "had been arcing" should read "arced."

The wrong tense can cause vertigo in readers. A story in *Rail Travel News* about a cross-country train trip stated: "We passed some empty cattle pens which were full of mooing cattle ..." *What?* wondered I, my mind reeling. I went back to the beginning of the sentence and started reading again. "We passed some empty cattle pens which were full of mooing cattle on some earlier trips over this route." It should have said, "... which had been full of mooing cattle on some earlier trips over this route."

Here's a rule of thumb* used by many editors: If you need to read something twice to understand it, then it needs editing.

Accuracy

Editors should demand accuracy. Since we are in the business of communication, we should insist that, as much as possible, the work we produce be true and correct.

Readers may not so much demand accuracy as presume it. This is all the more reason to be sure that we provide it. "The very act of printing something gives it the aura of authenticity," stated the *Editor's Workshop* newsletter. "And so accuracy must be sought and protected for even the most ephemeral of printing."[98]

Sources insist on accuracy, too. If we or the writers whose work we edit are ever quoted, we want to be quoted correctly, so accuracy is a courtesy in addition to being a responsibility.

"We [MacNeil and I] both believed that Getting It Right was the first rule of journalism," wrote Jim Lehrer, co-host of the *MacNeil-Lehrer NewsHour*, in his memoir *A Bus of My Own*. "And the second, the third, the fourth, and all the way to the tenth. Sloppiness with little facts, items as little even as middle initials or titles, leads to sloppiness with the big facts, the big ideas and most everything else. Reporters and editors who use or permit imprecise language, imperfect sourcing, sweeping

---

* I learned this one from Margaret Palm.

generalities, sarcasm, cheap shots and smug morality in straight news stories should be run out of the business …"[99]

"Too often … journalism crosses the line into melodramatic exaggeration," wrote Ed Jones, editor of the Fredericksburg, Virginia, *Free Lance-Star*.[100]

Michael Gerson of the *Washington Post* lamented a decline in media standards.

> Most cable news networks have forsaken objectivity entirely and produce little actual news … Most Internet sites display an endless hunger to comment and little appetite for verification. Free markets, it turns out, often make poor fact-checkers …
>
> Cable and the Internet now allow Americans, if they choose, to get their information entirely from sources that agree with them—sources that reinforce and exaggerate their political predispositions.[101]

Looking for support rather than truth is not proper research.

There are at least three good reasons for being zealous about accuracy: professionalism, credibility, and business.[102]

If communication is your vocation and not just an assignment, then you should desire to communicate well and not just adequately. Professionalism means doing the best job possible even if some (or even all) of the people you serve do not appreciate the level of quality.

Credibility means that people will trust what you have to say and turn to you for information. Botch a quotation, repeat hearsay as fact, or skew your meaning with misplaced jargon or double negatives, and you may have a big job ahead trying to rebuild your credibility. If you're in the information business, credibility is crucial. People won't pay you to provide information if you can't assemble and present facts accurately.

Accuracy pays, and inaccuracy can cost you. I recall an internal business memo that noted the loss of a client—and the client's name was misspelled. Maybe there was a connection.

Don't sacrifice your professionalism or lose your credibility or your business. Follow Jim Lehrer's rules 1 through 10: Get it right.

Make Sure the Author Has the Quotations Right

Editors must make sure that writers, in quoting from written material, follow the original quote precisely in terms of spelling, capitalization, and punctuation.

Quotations are indicated by quotation marks or block indention—that is, by indenting the entire quotation from the left margin or from both margins.

Any alterations made in a written quotation must be acknowledged. Notes within the text must be enclosed in brackets, not parentheses (an exception is Associated Press style). Emphasis added, such as italics, should be noted after the quotation unless this would mean placing the note at a great distance from the alteration.

In transcribing quotations received orally (from an interview or a broadcast, for example) the writer should use proper spelling and punctuation; emphasis may be added without comment if the words were clearly emphasized by the speaker.

"Can You Edit a Direct Quotation?" asked the title of an article in *The Editorial Eye*.[103]

"No," responded Bill Walsh, copy desk chief of *The Washington Times*. "If a 'problem' quote is the best one to tell the story, ellipses, bracketed inserts, and the partial-quote device are always available. ... 'Quote' means 'quote.' Writers have word after word after word at their disposal outside quotation marks; they have no business inserting their own prose inside them."

"Yes," answered Linda Jorgensen of *The Editorial Eye*. "We should have a good reason for editing a quote, and we should have an equally good reason for using one unedited if it might be embarrassing."

"Never alter quotations even to correct minor grammatical errors or word usage ..." says *The Associated Press Stylebook and Libel Manual*.[104] "Remember that you can misquote someone by giving a startling remark without its modifying passage or qualifiers. The manner of delivery sometimes is part of the context. Reporting a smile or a deprecatory gesture may be as important as conveying the words themselves."

I respect Linda Jorgensen's opinion, but I agree with Bill Walsh and the Associated Press: "Never alter quotations." It follows that what comes between quotation marks must be the speaker's or writer's exact words; scrutiny of quotations for words the speaker would not have said will turn up misquotations.

If you have a spoken error or misstatement in an interview transcript, though, you might be able to ask the speaker, "Did you mean to say ...?" Then you might obtain a new and better quotation.

Errors due to formatting, however, need not be reproduced in a quotation. A story that begins with a decorative capital letter in print can lose the first letter when the document is posted on a website or converted to text. When the result is a story beginning with the word "fghanistan," I have taken the liberty of supplying the missing *A*. Likewise I have deleted the hyphen when quoting an online document with the word *Afghanis-tan*. I was confident that the hyphen was a formatting error.

Also, editors need to recognize when a writer may have misheard something. Copy editor Laura Moyer cited a quotation in which *boom* should have been *boon*. "I'm not sure I could have heard a difference; these words sound so similar one could easily be misheard for the other," she wrote.[105] Another case she cited was *honing in* vs. *homing in*.

> Regardless of whether the story subject said "honing" or "homing," the reporter should have written "homing." And when the reporter didn't, an editor should have asked the reporter about it and negotiated a way to bring across meaning without embarrassing the speaker or ourselves.
>
> The options, as always:
>
> Paraphrase, taking the problematic word or phrase out of quotation marks.
>
> Or, if the reporter acknowledges that the error could have been his or hers, just change it.[106]

Another common problem related to quotations is dangling references or citations. As information added to a quotation, they are often mishandled.

What seems to mislead some writers is that, even though a citation is extraneous to a quotation, it still must be part of a sentence—we write in complete sentences. Or should.

Dangling references or citations must be outside the quotation marks or block indention, or else enclosed in brackets. For example:

> **Right:** "For God so loved the world ..." (John 3:16).
> **Wrong:** "For God so loved the world ... (John 3:16)."
> **Right:** "For God so loved the world ... [John 3:16]."

Ellipsis points are always three periods with space in between: They indicate something omitted or incomplete. In fact, they form one punctuation mark, and in most word-processing and page-layout software they are available as such (which prevents them from splitting at the end of a line). If they follow a sentence, keep the end-of-sentence punctuation before the ellipsis points. (See "Ellipsis Points" in chapter five.)

Block indention indicates that everything indented is part of a quote. Any notation made within the indented material must be enclosed in brackets. Material within block indention does not need quotation marks, except to indicate quotations within the whole quote.

Quotations from poetry call for extra caution on the part of editors— and poetry is more common than one might suppose. Much of the dialogue in Shakespeare's plays and large portions in some translations of the Bible (Psalms and prophecies, for example) are rendered in verse, and the poetry should be preserved in transcription. Poetry, when quoted, should, if possible, be set line for line (that is, with a new line beginning at every place where one occurs in the original poem). Take the example of Isaiah 60:1 in the Revised Standard Version of the Bible. Reproduced line for line, it would read:

> Arise, shine; for your light has come,
> and the glory of the LORD has risen upon you.

If there isn't room to set poetry line for line, or if it needs to be run into a paragraph, a slash can be used to indicate the line breaks in the original poem: "Arise, shine; for your light has come,/and the glory of the LORD has risen upon you."

In the above quotation, LORD appears in the Revised Standard Version of the Bible with a capital *L* and small capitals for ORD. It is important to preserve this, because some Bible versions use "cap-and-small" (that is, capitals plus small capitals) to indicate places where the original Hebrew text used the consonants of the name of God.

Don't confuse instances such as this with decorative initials or words that may open chapters. When quoted, these can be set normally.

Some Bible editions use italics when a word is contextually implied but does not actually appear in the original Hebrew or Greek; this information about the translation, if it is important to the readers, should be preserved and explained.

Titles referred to in text, notes, or a bibliography are usually set in initial caps—that is, nouns, verbs, pronouns, adjectives, and adverbs are capitalized. When citing titles, follow a standard format, not necessarily the typography on a book cover or in the title of a magazine article, which might have some oddball graphic treatment. For example, a book by Bernard Brodie has the entire title in lowercase letters on the front cover: *a guide to naval strategy*. If the book is mentioned in someone else's writing, the title should be capitalized in the normal manner: *A Guide to Naval Strategy*.

Whether to use italics for a title depends on what style guide you are following. The rules set forth in *Words Into Type* are typical (generally, italicize long works, such as books, plays, and series, and use quotation marks for shorter pieces, such as articles and poems).

Verify Copied Quotations

Quoted material in manuscripts generally is placed there in one of two ways: The author (1) typed it or (2) copied and pasted it. In either case, an editor needs to be on guard for errors in quotations. The editor should ask the author to supply copies of the sources—photocopies of book pages or a magazine article, for example, or electronic copies of (and links to) material found online; web pages can usually be saved as web archive (.mht) files, and many online documents are in Portable Document Format (PDF). Carelessly copying content from web pages or PDFs may scoop up footnote reference numbers, bibliographical reference numbers, and so on. Even if a source's internal citations are going to be reproduced in a quotation, they probably won't use the same numbering, and the author, editor, and proofreader need to be careful to reproduce them accurately and distinguish quoted footnotes from the author's own. (When footnote reference numbers appear in the text without accompanying footnotes in the margins, it may be a tipoff that something was plagiarized—copied and pasted without permission or attribution.)

Use "Sic" Properly

Sometimes it is necessary to let the reader know that what looks like an error in a quotation is in fact correct. This usually applies to misspellings or variant spellings, or to missing words or punctuation. It tells the reader, "This is not a mistake; it is quoted correctly."

In *Against the Grain* magazine, an article by Randy Engel called "Why the Population Council Is a Rockefeller Baby" (John D. Rockefeller III was its first president, in case you're wondering) provides an instance where *sic* should have been used if the mistake was in the original.

> The Population Council received an AID grant … "to develop a non-toxic and completely effective substance or method that when self-administered on a single occasion would ensure the nonpregnant sate at completion of one monthly cycle."

If the original actually said *sate* instead of *state*, that should be noted. Instead it leaves the reader with the impression, probably correct, that the quotation was incorrectly transcribed or poorly proofread, or maybe both.

But unnecessary use of *sic* sounds self-righteous and prideful. Other people's mistakes should be pointed out only when necessary to make sure that the reader gets the message, or if you are, for example, writing a book about editing. In *The First Salute* by Barbara Tuchman, we read, "At the home of Joseph Reed, 'President of the State [sic] of Pennsylvania,' the visitors are entertained at a ceremonial dinner …" That *sic* is Ms. Tuchman's, not mine. I'm not sure why it's there. Maybe she was calling attention to the fact that Pennsylvania is not officially a state but a commonwealth. That's not necessary; a reader is not likely to think that *State* is a typo. If that's not why she used *sic*, what was she emphasizing? If the error in the original isn't obvious, then the reader needs an explanation of what was said and why it was wrong.

Make Sure the Author Keeps the Facts Straight

Unless a work is total fantasy, such as *The Lord of the Rings*, the author will be incorporating facts from the real world. Even fantasy needs to be consistent within itself: Facts need to match up, even if they're imaginary facts (such as the geography of Middle-earth). "Only by thoughtful concentration on details can fiction be satisfactorily edited," states *Words Into Type*.[107]

In many cases, the editor must presume that the writer is knowledgeable. As that verb suggests, this can be presumptuous. Editors, therefore, must be on the lookout for blunders, especially in areas outside the author's expertise. It helps to have experts available who can read manuscripts to verify their accuracy.

In one book I edited, the author kept referring to the social upper crust of Hong Kong during the 1930s as "the jet set." ("Jet set" was a 1950s term; there were no commercial jets in the 1930s.)

On her Red Pen blog, Laura Moyer, a newspaper copy editor, noted some factual errors she spotted.[108]

- "Beijing, the only nation that requires couples to have only one child" (Beijing is not a nation and doesn't require couples to have any children).
- "Dallas beat the Mavericks" (the Mavericks are the Dallas team).
- "The particles with a positive charge are called electrons" (electrons have a negative charge).

Experience has led me to follow a double rule: (1) When in doubt, look it up, and (2) doubt everything. Publishers somewhere may still employ full-time fact checkers. More often, the task of checking facts devolves upon the copy editor. The reason for doubting, and checking, everything possible is that authors, like editors, make mistakes, and you never know where the mistakes will crop up.

When editing, I verify everything I can. One reason is that I often uncover errors I wouldn't have suspected.

One article stated, "The New Madrid Earthquake was addressed in an exercise called CAT97." A quick online search revealed that there have been many earthquakes centered on a fault that passes through New Madrid, Missouri. My guess was that the exercise involved a hypothetical earthquake, not "the" New Madrid earthquake. I was right: CAT97 involved a hypothetical "catastrophic earthquake."

But there was more. On page three of the information from the Federal Emergency Management Agency, a paragraph began with this sentence: "CAT-97 is a seminar and not an exercise." So there was another error I wouldn't have guessed at. (As for the name, the agency was inconsistent about hyphenating "CAT-97.")

Here are three questions I submitted to a writer concerning one report. I had two pages of notes and questions, but these give an idea of the sorts of things that can go wrong.

- Note 30 consists only of a dead hyperlink. It needs a proper citation.
- Figure 7: Some items in the figure are followed by an asterisk, some by two asterisks, but there is only one note below the figure. Is a note missing? Is the figure wrong?
- Note 44 merely says, "Ibid.," indicating that the source is exactly the same as in the previous note, but the previous note does not name a source.

Some items are easy to check. If a manuscript includes addresses or phone numbers, make sure they're up to date. I once published a magazine article sidebar containing the addresses of four organizations, drawing the information from the organizations' letterheads. By the time the sidebar was published, three of the four organizations had moved, so the sidebar that appeared in the magazine was 75 percent wrong. Since then I have made it a point to verify all addresses and phone numbers before publishing them.

One report I edited cited a Senate hearing involving "Commerce, Science and Technology"; I didn't know whether this was correct, so I checked the Senate website to verify it. The actual name is the Commerce, Science, and Transportation Committee. Then I looked up the actual hearing to make sure it involved the full committee (it did) and not a subcommittee with *technology* in the name. Two other errors in the same report were easily checked: Janet Napolitano's title was Secretary of Homeland Security (or Homeland Security Secretary), not Secretary of the Department of Homeland Security, and the GAO is the Government Accountability Office (it changed its name from "General Accounting Office" in 2004). Maybe these would qualify as those ingenious saves that Brendan Gill credited to editors. Still, "publishers say that responsibility for errors and fabrications ultimately must lie with the author," wrote Motoko Rich in *The New York Times*.[109]

Copy editor and Red Pen blogger Laura Moyer described her reaction to a grammar gaffe in her Red Pen newspaper column: "I tell myself what I tell others: If you don't want a mistake to appear under your byline, don't put it there. If an editor corrects a mistake and saves your bacon, say thanks and know that you were lucky."[110]

Check the Math

Well, check the math if you can. I have edited documents in which the math was way over my head. In those cases, and in other cases that didn't involve math, I had to trust the author to get it right. However, there are numerous cases in which some elementary arithmetic can determine that something does not add up, as in this statement about the Homeland Security Advisory System: "The five levels are Low, Guarded, Elevated, and High." As you can see, that adds up to only four, not five, levels. That's why my editorial checklist says, "Check all arithmetic. Make sure that columns of numbers add up if they are supposed to. Make sure that pie charts total 100 percent." They often do not.

Statements about numbers may be suspect, too. "Sales of retail properties in the Puget Sound region" for "the 1996-97 fiscal year ... totaled $307," stated the *Puget Sound Business Journal* for the week of February 28, 2000. It's possible, but it's more likely that the writer left out some zeroes or a word such as *million*.

Sometimes numbers are plainly wrong but an editor can't tell what they should be. One report I edited said that a network was supposed "to reach 140% or 150% of the population." Another network supposedly had "5.268,3000 million subscribers."

Once I was editing a document and came to a "top ten" list. Based on experience, the first thing I did was to count the items on the list. There were only nine. I took it to the typesetter who had been working with the author, and I said we needed to find out from the author what the tenth item should be. No, she told me, the document had been in production for months, and the author was very slow to answer queries. She changed the list heading to "Top Nine."

Another common numerical error involves misuse of words, such as *decimate* ("reduce by one-tenth," though often used loosely nowadays) or, possibly the most abused mathematical word these days, *exponential*.[111] Doubling won't do. Tripling is tedious. Nowadays, the only growth worthy of respect is exponential.

A June 1999 press release from the U.S. Census Bureau claimed "Exponential Growth in Number of Centenarians": "The number of centenarians in the U.S. is growing rapidly ... During the 1990s, the ranks of centenarians nearly doubled, from about 37,000 counted at the start of the decade to more than an estimated 70,000." However, as math teacher and analyst Kristin Lynch pointed out, "Doubling is not exponential growth."

Math League Multimedia[112] explains that "exponential notation is useful in situations where the same number is multiplied repeatedly. The number being multiplied is called the base, and the exponent tells how many times the base is multiplied by itself." If the Census Bureau were right, what would the exponent be? If 37,000 had been multiplied by itself even once (37,000²), the product would have been 1.369 billion, not 70,000. Another decade of exponential growth and people over one hundred would far outnumber everyone who had ever lived on Earth.* Too bad the Census Bureau didn't specify the exponent.

Numerical errors can be costly failures to communicate the right information. "A missing zero on its Internet sites" in December 2002 threatened "to cost hotel giant Starwood either a lot of money or some customer goodwill," reported *USA Today*.[113] The website "showed $85 rates—instead of $850—for over-the-water bungalows during high season at its luxurious new resort on the French Polynesian island of Bora Bora in the South Pacific.

"Over two days, 136 people booked 2,631 rooms at the cheap rate and some made multiple reservations covering more than two months of vacation, Starwood says. If all the reservations were kept, the glitch would cost the resort $2 million." It wasn't the first time for Starwood, either. A year earlier, the company's site had advertised—and honored—room rates of $0 at its W Times Square hotel in New York City. The story cited other costly pricing errors on corporate websites, such as United Airlines' charging $25 for San Francisco–Paris flights and $5 for Chicago–Denver flights.

Obviously editors need to check monetary figures closely; likewise statistics. "Editors should take a close look at any statistic and be especially skeptical of projections, not just to find typos but also to find errors—or bias—in analysis," said editor Dave Fessenden.

Even if the statistic is technically true, it may tend to communicate misinformation. A 2005 story in the *Honolulu Star-Bulletin* about the University of Hawaii's study of processed meats said that people who ate large amounts of processed meat had a two-thirds higher rate of pancreatic cancer.[114] That's true as far as it goes. But the rest of the numbers are not so scary: The university studied 190,545 men and women for seven

---

* An exponent doesn't have to be a whole number: $37,000^{1.06}$ is approximately 70,000. At that relatively slow exponential rate, it would take more than a century for the number of centenarians to exceed a billion.

years, and "there were 482 cases of pancreatic cancer." That's a quarter of 1 percent. So if the hot dog gobblers were two-thirds as likely as the others to develop pancreatic cancer, it still indicates that fewer than half of 1 percent of them got the disease.

Make Sure the Author Attributes Borrowed Ideas to Proper Sources

I once found an author claiming that "good is the enemy of best," meaning that settling for something that is merely good can prevent someone from reaching the highest level of achievement. The book was intended to be inspirational, and it liberally quoted from the Bible, so I looked in a topical concordance for references to *good* as a substantive and found that "the good" was always endorsed and even attributed to God. I altered the author's comments to make it clear that "good" itself is not a hindrance but that settling for too little can be. Unfortunately there was another problem that was not apparent until much later.

When editing another author's book, I found that same statement: "Good is the enemy of best." It was a short leap to the conclusion that the idea was not original with either author.

Much later I discovered[115] Voltaire's statement "Le mieux est l'ennemi du bien" ("The best is the enemy of the good" or, more precisely, "The best thing is the enemy of the good thing")—a point well taken and a good contrast to the claim that "good is the enemy of best."

Unoriginal writing is bad enough; plagiarism is worse. It can be blatant, such as an author (a college professor, no less) lifting entire paragraphs from another source; I once received an author's column and found that portions of it were remarkably similar—in fact, identical—to portions of another writer's column that had appeared in print a short while before.

Unfortunately a good deal of plagiarism probably slips past editors. Writers of integrity (and there are many) will not intentionally borrow anyone else's ideas or words without giving credit. Standard publishing contracts require the author to warrant that the entire work, excepting portions specifically identified, is the author's original creation. However, editors and publishers prefer to catch plagiarism—intentional or unintentional—before it gets into print. One of the few safeguards is to be well-read, so as to catch borrowed words or ideas. Another is to have each manuscript reviewed by one or more experts in the appropriate field before publication. This is standard practice with scholarly, peer-reviewed journals, but plagiarism or even fraud is not unknown even in those.

Plagiarism can occur inadvertently, too. "The *San Francisco Chronicle's Book Review* ... printed, under one man's byline, a review that proved to have been largely lifted from a review by another man published in the *Washington Post's Book World*," reported *The Editorial Eye*.[116] A reviewer downloaded the *Book World* review to study it, and while the reviewer was out of town, the book review editor retrieved it and printed it, thinking it was a review by the *Chronicle's* own staff member.

Another possibility for inadvertent plagiarism lies in transcriptions of spoken words. A speaker might indicate a quotation by using a different tone of voice, which might not be noted in a transcription. "I've caught a few of these unattributed quotes, so I suspect there are probably a few others I've missed," said editor Dave Fessenden. Listening to a recording of the spoken words (if one is available) provides a safeguard in this area.

There also can, at times, be a fine line between allusion and plagiarism. While an author certainly may use ideas and phrases that literate readers will recognize as allusions to the work of well-known writers, the editor should take care that obscure or extensive allusion will not be mistaken for the author's own, original comments. The safest course, when in doubt, is to credit the source within the text or in a note.

Make Sure the Author Used Reliable Sources

It is worthwhile for an editor to keep an eye on the author's sources. If the author is claiming objectivity, did the writer consult conflicting and opposing sources? Or consult any primary sources?

In 2006, *The Manila Times* (Philippines) advised the Heritage Foundation that it "should not use only secondary materials," taking issue with "the section on the Philippines in the 2006 Index of

Economic Freedom, published by the Heritage Foundation"; the newspaper said that the index was "full of errors, some egregious, making its value, not to speak of its utility, suspect."[117] If the newspaper's comments are accurate, they make for a cautionary note about "open-source research," which could actually be secondhand research.

The behemoth of open-source research is Wikipedia. Among its "central tenets: articles must reflect a neutral point of view ... and their content must be both verifiable and previously published," wrote Stacy Schiff in *The New Yorker*. Wikipedia has a "prohibition against original research."[118]

Philip Roth, in another *New Yorker* piece, wrote that "the Wikipedia entry discussing" his novel *The Human Stain* contained "a serious misstatement." Yet when he "petitioned Wikipedia to delete this misstatement, along with two others," he was told, through a third party, that he, "Roth, was not a credible source," and that Wikipedia requires secondary sources.[119]

Schiff described another case.

> William Connolley, a climate modeller at the British Antarctic Survey, in Cambridge, was briefly a victim of an edit war over the entry on global warming, to which he had contributed ... Connolley believes that Wikipedia "gives no privilege to those who know what they're talking about" ...
>
> Eric Raymond, the open-source pioneer whose work inspired [Wikipedia founder Jimmy] Wales ... believes that the open-source model is simply inapplicable to an encyclopedia.[120]

"It's impossible to know whether the entry you're reading has been most recently edited by a true expert in the field or by Bozo the Vengeful Clown," wrote Evan Morris, the Word Detective.[121]

Certainly Wikipedia has flaws, but it has its defenders, too. It "has long been the best encyclopedia available in English ..." wrote Maria Bustillos in 2011. "It's been over five years since the landmark study in *Nature* that showed 'few differences in accuracy' between Wikipedia and the *Encyclopedia Britannica.* ... Wikipedia has three main advantages over its print ancestors:[122]

1. Wikipedia offers far richer, more comprehensive citations to source materials and bibliographies on- and offline, thereby providing a far better entry point for serious study;
2. It is instantly responsive to new developments;
3. Most significantly, users can "look under the hood" of Wikipedia in order to investigate the controversial or doubtful aspects of any given subject.[123]

Still, Wikipedia, Bustillos noted, is only a starting point for research: "No undergraduate paper should be citing *any encyclopedia whatsoever.*"[124] Nor, I would add, should any credible author of a book or article.

That's "almost always true," said editor Dave Fessenden. "But just as an author may cite a dictionary definition of a word such as *love* as an introduction to an essay on love, I can see an encyclopedia being referenced" for basic facts.

Editors should insist on reliable sources and should adjure authors to leave out what they are unsure of. One book manuscript I worked on asserted that scientists say bumblebees can't fly; whatever scientist (if any) had made this statement wasn't cited. Bumblebees (supposedly) fly because they don't know they can't. I recommended that the author drop this claim about bumblebees' inability to fly.

Soon afterward, I found another author asserting that bumblebees can't fly and concluded that both authors were probably repeating from memory something they had heard. Editors should recommend that writers cite facts from memory only when the memories originate from their own experiences; even then, it's best for a writer to rely on notes or journals. Facts outside the author's experience or area of expertise should be obtained from reliable sources, and those sources should be cited.

This was before Barry Siskind's 2001 book *Bumblebees Can't Fly*, an advertising blurb for which said, "When bumblebees ignore science and take off in flight, they're using common sense."

In *Science News Online*, Ivars Peterson commented on the claim that bumblebees can't fly.[125]

> It apparently first surfaced in Germany in the 1930s, and the story was about a prominent Swiss aerodynamicist. One evening at dinner, the researcher happened to be talking to a biologist, who asked about the flight of bees. To answer the biologist's query, the Swiss engineer did a quick "back-of-the-napkin" calculation.
>
> To keep things simple, he assumed a rigid, smooth wing, estimated the bee's weight and wing area, and calculated the lift generated by the wing. Not surprisingly, there was insufficient lift. That was about all he could do at a dinner party. The detailed calculations had to wait.
>
> To the biologist, however, the aerodynamicist's initial failure was sufficient evidence of the superiority of nature to mere engineering. The story spread, told from the biologist's point of view, and it wasn't long before it started to appear in magazine and newspaper articles.
>
> Unfortunately, the wrong lesson emerged from the story. The real issue is not that scientists are wrong but that there's a crucial difference between a thing and a mathematical model of the thing.

His words offer some food for thought where editing is concerned. They should remind us of Alfred Korzybski's statement "The map is not the territory," a proverb among semanticists. Not only are there differences between things and their representation, but between hearsay and facts, and between secondhand quotations and original sources.

The Homework Spot website[126] offers guidance for evaluating the trustworthiness of a website. "The World Wide Web is like a virtual library, with one major difference," it says. "… On the Web, anyone can publish."[127]

> Before you start looking for information, carefully select your source. The Internet is not always the best place to begin. Ask yourself the following questions:

- What kind of information am I looking for?
- Which sources would be the most helpful in finding that information?

The site lists some questions to ask.

- "Is the author's name listed, along with his/her email or street address? If no one takes credit for the work, its accuracy may be questionable."
- "What are the author's qualifications?"
- "Who is responsible for the site …?"
- "Is the information current? What is the 'last revised' date on the page?"
- "Does the site have a lot of dead links?"
- "Does the information seem slanted in any way, indicating a bias that is unfair or unsupported?"
- "Does the site have spelling and grammar errors? (Signs of carelessness)."
- "Has the site been given an award or high rating by a reputable group?"[128]

Distrust Secondhand Quotes

A question submitted to Garson O'Toole, the Quote Investigator, follows: "The depth and breadth of information available on the internet is wondrous, but why is there so much junk and misinformation about quotations? The prevalence of inaccurate data makes it harder to find correct information."[129]

In 2009, a fake quotation from composer Maurice Jarre "was invented by an Irish student who posted it on the Wikipedia website in a hoax designed to show the dangers of relying too heavily on the Internet for information," reported Reuters. "Shane Fitzgerald … said he had expected blogs and perhaps small newspapers to use the quotes but did not believe major publications would rely on Wikipedia without further checks."

Journalists "'shouldn't use information they find [on Wikipedia] if it can't be traced back to a reliable primary source,' said the [London] *Guardian*'s readers' editor Siobhain Butterworth."[130]

Secondhand quotations tend to be like the game of Telephone, in which a message is passed along a chain of people and usually gets hopelessly distorted along the way. "In some cases, it's a simple question of word order," wrote Maria Konnikova. "… In some, it's a simplification or contraction of something that's a bit messier to remember without it." Others "are more perfidious and sneaky. The famous 'power corrupts; absolute power corrupts absolutely,' for one, diverges in just one tiny way from Lord Acton's original phrasing: 'Power tends to corrupt; absolute power corrupts absolutely.' … Rhetorically, the first one surely sounds better (hence, our enhanced memory of it and taste for its correctness). But the gulf between it and the real thing is vast."[131] Today, she pointed out, virtually any quotation can be tracked to its original source.

Garson O'Toole, the Quote Investigator, generously does this, often finding that quotations popularly attributed to famous figures (typically Albert Einstein, Mark Twain, Abraham Lincoln, or Winston Churchill) were really said by somebody else. "Some people think that Albert Einstein's name is magical," he wrote. "If they want to convince you of something or sell you something they invoke his revered name to prove that a genius agrees with whatever proposition they are peddling."[132]

One book I edited contained not only secondhand quotations but a third-hand quotation. When I questioned parts of the manuscript, the author replied with drawings of donkey heads (representing me) and generally refused to provide documentation.

One of the supposed quotations was from *Linacre Quarterly*, in turn supposedly quoting a book, *The Thanatos Syndrome* by Walker Percy. The article in *Linacre Quarterly* had mistakenly included an editorial comment in a block-indented quotation from the book and had added two words to the quotation.

Attempting to quote from that article, the author who draws donkey heads had preserved *Linacre Quarterly*'s errors and added new ones, inserting his own comments in parentheses, removing all paragraph breaks, changing ellipsis points to a period, and omitting a quotation mark. Finally, yet another typist got involved, adding even more errors.

I was able to untangle the mess only by borrowing *The Thanatos Syndrome* from the library and looking up the quotation myself.

It is amazing how many writers today cannot transcribe a quotation without making a mistake. Hence the need for the author and the editor to use primary sources. I usually request that authors provide copies of everything they have quoted.

There are, as well, a few trustworthy secondary sources.

The *Oxford Dictionary of Quotations* and *Bartlett's Familiar Quotations* are authoritative and unimpeachable sources—generally. In his book *On Language*,[133] William Safire recorded an exchange of correspondence with one of his readers, Hamilton A. Long of Philadelphia. Safire had attributed to Edmund Burke the statement "The only thing necessary for the triumph of evil is for good men to do nothing." Long wrote to Safire, asking when and where Burke had said that. Safire turned to *Bartlett's*, where the statement was indeed cited as existing in a letter written by Burke. Long said that the citation was false. Inquiries to the British Library and the Library of Congress proved it false, failing to turn up the statement anywhere in Burke's writings.

The need for accurate quotation and citations leads into the topic of bibliographies, which we will discuss next.

Beneficial Bibliographies[134]

Bibliographies can be intimidating to reader and writer alike. They can turn into babel and fail to communicate. To succeed at communication, the author and editor need to keep the reader in mind.

To be useful, a bibliographic citation must provide enough information for the reader to find the work being referenced. How much detail to give depends on the work and where it may be found. For a book, the author, title, publisher, city of publication, and date are basic; with this information, a librarian can turn up almost any title. There is a good deal of overlap in the names of books, authors, and even publishers, so the date and city may be necessary to identify a book. If there is more than one edition or volume, these should be given as well.

If the reader is likely to obtain the book from a store rather than a library, the International Standard Book Number (ISBN) should be provided, because many stores use it to order titles. If specific material within a book is cited, the page numbers should be included, too.

Citations of periodicals should include the author, article title, volume and issue numbers, date, and page number(s).

Citations of information published on the Internet should include the Internet address plus the name of the website and page in case the address changes. Electronic documents can include a link to the referenced site.

Whether to place bibliographic notes at the end of a chapter or at the end of a book, or as footnotes on the page depends on when the reader needs the information, but full citations in the text rarely increase readability. Nevertheless I think it's good to provide some information about the source. "Smith, 1996" is an acceptable in-text citation in scientific writing, because the reader can easily find the corresponding entry in the bibliography. By itself, though, this type of citation says nothing about the source's identity or credibility—and further, I've often come across in-text citations that *weren't* in the bibliography. Then it can be impossible for an editor to verify the entry. "Smith, 1996" doesn't give you much to go on. A phrase like "As Albert Smith wrote in *Bibliography Babel* ... " (I made that up) at least says that Smith is the author of a book on the subject.

What about the format of citations? You can follow something as complex as Chicago style, which contains more than 150 pages on bibliographic citations, or as simple as the three-page "Documentation of Sources" section in the back of *Merriam-Webster's Collegiate Dictionary*. Whichever style you choose, using one format, with the information in the same order for every entry, makes it easier for the reader to decipher.

Many other questions will arise: Should the number of a government report be included? If a journal article has six authors, should they all be listed? Is it okay to use abbreviations of Latin terms (*ibid.*, *op. cit.*, *et al.*)? The answers always depend on another question: What will be most useful to the reader? For instance, "'I.e.' and 'e.g.' are among the most commonly misused abbreviations in English. ..." according to Evan Morris, the Word Detective.

> "I.e." stands for "id est," which means, simply, "that is" or "which is to say." ...
>
>> "E.g." is an abbreviation of "exempli gratia," which means "for example" or "for instance."
>
>> I must now add a caution. The point of writing is to be read, and if you think that there is even a middling chance that your audience will not understand "i.e." or "e.g.," don't use them.[135]

Truth, Fiction, or Falsehood?

Occasionally an editor may be assigned work in which accuracy is the least of the author's—or even the publisher's—concerns. In deciding where to draw the line (it may become the unemployment line), editors may wish to consider the following discussion of what constitutes a lie, excerpted from *The Language Maven Strikes Again* by William Safire.[136]

> English clergyman Robert South: "A *lye* is properly an outward signification of something contrary to, or at least beside, the inward sense of the mind; so that when one thing is signified or expressed, and the same thing not meant, or intended, that is properly a *lye*." ...
>
>> This advice from the poet William Blake may serve: "A truth that's told with bad intent/ Beats all the lies you can invent." ...
>
>>> I suggest that the act of lying is but one type of misrepresenting behavior and requires the following conditions to be met:

i. Some "fact" is asserted (not implied, entailed, or presupposed)

ii. The speaker believes the fact to be untrue (knowledge not required)

iii. The assertion is made with intent to deceive.

Bruce Fraser
Professor of Linguistics
Boston University
Boston, Massachusetts

William Lutz, author of *The New Doublespeak*, "believes that 'the irresponsible use of language strikes at the very core of an ordered, just and virtuous society,'" according to book reviewer Mary Stoughton. "Lutz turns to Dante for metaphor and notes that in his Hell, 'the worst sinners are the fraudulent, those who misuse language to mislead and deceive.'"[137]

Questions of truth and lies are not always clear-cut, however. "Newspapers don't seem to know whether they're supposed to be observers who document what happens before their eyes or analysts who connect the dots in all of what reporters see, read and hear," commented *Washington Post* ombudsman Joann Byrd, who added parenthetically, "Journalism is going through a transition period, and it does not help that readers are evenly divided about which they expect."[138]

Copyright, Permission, and Fair Use

Facts aren't copyrighted, but ideas and information obtained by the author must be credited to their sources. A writer may report news learned elsewhere as long as the source is credited and any direct quotations are clearly identified. Nearly all other writing is automatically protected by copyright law. Most government documents are exceptions.

Fair use is governed by precedent, translated into general rules. Usually small portions of a copyrighted work may be reproduced without permission. However, the excerpt must not reproduce the substance of something. Copying small portions of a book or magazine article is usually considered fair use. However, copying half a news item is not.

Even one line of poetry or song lyrics may capture the substance of the work, so reproducing these things almost always requires permission. When in doubt, get permission.

The question of how much you may reproduce is linked in copyright law to how it affects the market for the original source. "Quoting and paraphrasing all the main points of another book" probably crosses the line and harms its sales, even if not much of it is directly quoted, wrote editor Dave Fessenden in his book *Concept to Contract.*[139]

Copyrights do expire: They have limited, varying terms, depending on when the copyright was established and whether it was renewed. Once they expire, they pass into the public domain (that is, public ownership). At that point they may be reproduced freely, though credit to the author should still be given. Please note: Public domain is not the same as public availability. Open-source material is what can be obtained publicly without restriction; that doesn't mean it's publicly owned. On the contrary, unless it is a government document or very old, it is likely protected by copyright, and the rules about fair use apply.

5

Editing for Grammar

The diction, grammar, and rhetoric of the writer are subject to critical inspection. The editor has learned from experience that the possibilities of error are limitless.

—Words Into Type[140]

Although most writers and editors have received extensive training in written English, and may even have attended something we used to call grammar school, we still make mistakes—all the time.

"Newspapers exasperate thousands of English teachers every day," said *Washington Post* ombudsman Joann Byrd, "as they set bad examples and hide their respect for the language. Even so literate a newspaper as *The Post* lands on the doorstep with words misspelled, homonyms scrambled and syntax in disarray."[141]

The Careful Writer, Words Into Type, The Elements of Style, and other sources offer voluminous instruction and examples for writers and editors. It is my intention simply to address some problems I often encounter.

Parts of Speech

Distinguishing Nouns and Verbs From Adjectives, Adverbs, and Other Modifiers

Some writers confuse adjectives with verb phrases. *Pickup* is an adjective, as in "a pickup game of softball," or a noun, as in "driving a pickup." *Pick up* is a verb phrase: a verb actually made up of two words—a verb and an adverb—in a phrase. Typically, the noun and adjective forms are one word, whereas the verbs are phrases—two or more words.

Wrong: "Pickup the paper off the floor."
Right: "Pick up the paper off the floor."

Wrong: "The start up costs are too high."
Right: "The startup costs are too high."

Wrong: "The game is setup and ready to play."
Right: "The game is set up and ready to play."

Wrong: "That is our fall back position."
Right: "That is our fallback position."

In these cases, pay attention to pronunciation and word usage to determine whether it is an adjective or verb phrase. When in doubt, check the dictionary.

Unclear Antecedents and Other Relationship Problems

"'Byng was duly shot by a firing squad of brother officers for no discernible purpose except to encourage the others,' as remarked by a mean-minded Frenchman. Voltaire's comment would immortalize the act ..." wrote Barbara Tuchman in *The First Salute*. Was Voltaire that mean-minded Frenchman, or was she alluding to another comment by Voltaire?

The relationships among words may be foggiest when pronouns are involved. "The antecedent of a pronoun should never be in doubt," states *Words Into Type*. The antecedent "must be expressed or clearly understood."[142] Remember that *such* can be a pronoun. Too often I find the phrase *as such* without an antecedent, prodding me to ask, often impatiently and out loud, "As *what*?" I'm reminded of the "caucus race" in *Alice's Adventures in Wonderland*.

> "Stigand, the patriotic archbishop of Canterbury, found it advisable—"
> "Found WHAT?" said the Duck.

Make sure your readers know what *it* means when it is used.

Copy editor Laura Moyer provided a good example of a dangling participle: "'After a long recovery and lowered activity level, the pounds started to add up.' … as written, the sentence says that 'the pounds' had a long recovery and lowered activity level."[143] The most important part—the person who experienced this—is left out. If the subject's name is Tiny, you could write, "Tiny found that after a long recovery and lowered activity level, the pounds started to add up."

Change of Person in Pronouns

"He slips in an interesting admission when he wonders if such action might make 'the enemy's thirst for peace be equal to our own,'" wrote Barbara Tuchman in *The First Salute*. Here a quotation was being used to complete a thought within a sentence. *He* is third person, but *our* is first person.

If first person is used in a third-person narrative, it should be in a quotation that links it directly to a speaker, not attached to a third-person pronoun. The problem could have been avoided by separating the third-person statement from the first-person quotation: "He slips in an interesting admission. Such action might make 'the enemy's thirst for peace be equal to our own,' he states."

Agreement of Pronouns, Verbs, and Antecedents

Pronouns have to match their verbs: We are. I am. You are. They are. It is. You get the idea.

I could stop right there, but a lot of writers don't get the idea, or at least they put onto paper things they would never say—unless, maybe, they were sportscasters. Sam McManis had this to say on the subject in a *San Francisco Chronicle* article.

> I must vent about a particularly grating linguistic tic from sportscasters that really ticks me off:

Pronoun-antecedent agreement.

We all learned it in fifth grade, right? Singular nouns take singular pronouns. And plural nouns take plural pronouns. Then there are the switch-hitters, "nouns of multitude," which change depending on the case and one's taste. This is English, so there always will be exceptions. ...

The other night, one of these sportscasters was showing highlights of the Stanford women's dismantling an early-round foe, and he said something like, "Stanford extended their lead ..."

Its. Stanford extended its lead, buddy.

This is called disagreement in number. Not to get overly pedantic, but an institution of higher learning is always singular. It is the school's team name that is plural. Of course, there are exceptions to that, too. ...

I KNOW, I know. Such picky stuff makes your hair hurt. Why not sit back and enjoy the game, bub? Because we have a sports-loving president who utters sentences such as, "Is our children learning?" That's why.[144]

Stanford is an *it*, not a *he, she,* or *they,* so there's no excuse in this case, but many people, to avoid using *he* or *she* or other pronouns of gender when the context implies neither male nor female, resort to using *they* and *their* as singular pronouns (as in "Every student must hand in their work on time.") As Sam McManis might say, "*Student* is singular, buddy."

His 'n' Her Pronouns[145]

People don't like to be dismissed with a pronoun. Miss Manners, for example, has said that she doesn't care to have the pronoun *nobody* applied to her—as in "Nobody cares about etiquette." Likewise it's unfair to write women or men out of a story by careless use of pronouns. Laura Moyer had this to say on the topic.

When a story refers to "a spokesperson" the person referred to is a woman. Every single time.

If it's a guy, reporters just write "spokesman." It's the most natural thing in the world.

A "chairperson," too, is always a woman. ...

Calling a man a man and a woman a person isn't sexism; in
a mixed-up way, it's the opposite. The reporter is trying so hard to
be non-sexist that he or she overcorrects and runs off the side of
the road.

It is OK to call a woman a woman. No offense taken, really.[146]

"Because language plays a central role in the way human beings think
and behave, we still need to promote language that opens rather than
closes possibilities for women and men," noted the National Council of
Teachers of English.[147]

"Women should receive the same treatment as men in all areas of
coverage," states *The Associated Press Stylebook*. "Physical descriptions,
sexist references, demeaning stereotypes and condescending phrases
should not be used." While acknowledging that "valid and acceptable
words such as *mankind* or *humanity*" may be used, the AP guide sets
forth some examples for its writers.

- "Copy should not assume maleness when both sexes are
  involved."
- "Copy should not express surprise that an attractive woman can
  be professionally accomplished."
- "Copy should not gratuitously mention family relationships
  when there is no relevance to the subject."
- "Use the same standards for men and women in deciding
  whether to include specific mention of personal appearance or
  marital and family situation."

However, applying these rules causes trouble for many writers and editors, because common answers to the problem, such as *he or she*, are not
everyday language. "Start using 'he or she' or 'his or her' in a conversa-
tion and people give you strange looks," noted editor Dave Fessenden.

"Sprinkling 'him/her' and 'his/her' through every paragraph is awkward and annoying and, consequently, is favored as a solution only by awkward and annoying writers," wrote Evan Morris, the Word Detective.[148]

The National Council of Teachers of English offered some practical alternatives.[149]

- Use "the same titles for men and women when naming jobs that could be held by both": instead of "chairman/chairwoman," use "chairperson" or "chair"; use "police officer" instead of "policeman/policewoman."

Noting that "there is no one pronoun in English that can be effectively substituted for" *he* or *his*, the English teachers suggested the following.[150]

- "Drop the possessive form altogether" or "substitute an article": Change "The average student is worried about his grades" to "The average student is worried about grades."
- "Use the plural instead of the singular": Change "Give the student his grade right away" to "Give the students their grades right away."
- Substitute the second or first person "for the third person": Change "When a teacher asks his students for an evaluation, he is putting himself on the spot" to "When you ask your students for an evaluation, you are putting yourself on the spot."
- The pronoun *one* or *one's* "can be substituted for" *he* or *his*, though it does change the tone: "He might well wonder what his response should be" could be changed to "One might well wonder what one's response should be."
- Recast the sentence "in the passive voice or another impersonal construction"—for example, change "Each student should hand in his paper promptly" to "Papers should be handed in promptly."
- "When the subject is an indefinite pronoun," recast the sentence to avoid it: Change "When everyone contributes his own ideas,

the discussion will be a success" to "When all the students contribute their own ideas, the discussion will be a success."

- Make sparing use of *he or she* and *his or her*—for example, change "Each student can select his own topic" to "Each student can select his or her own topic."

The English teachers also had a few things to say about occupational stereotyping.

- Avoid "diminutive or special forms to name women" (or men), such as "stewardess," "waitress," or "male nurse"; use "flight attendant," "server," and "nurse."
- Do not represent women or men "as occupying only certain jobs or roles": Don't assume that a kindergarten teacher is a she or that a pupil's mother would be the one preparing food.
- "Treat men and women in a parallel manner": Instead of "The class interviewed Chief Justice Burger and Mrs. O'Connor," write *The class interviewed Warren Burger and Sandra O'Connor* or *The class interviewed Chief Justice Burger and Justice O'Connor.*
- "Seek alternatives to language that patronizes or trivializes women" or "reinforces stereotyped images," such as "gal Friday," "career woman," or "man-sized job."

In addition, the teachers suggested ways to handle quotations that contain sexist language—without altering the quotations.

- "Avoid the quotation altogether if it is not really necessary."
- "Paraphrase the quotation, giving the original author credit for the idea."
- "If the quotation is fairly short, recast it as an indirect quotation, substituting nonsexist words as necessary."

Grammar checkers in software such as Microsoft Word can be set to catch gender-specific terms, but they tend to be weak on context. For example, Word objected to the phrase *military men and women*, pointing out that *men* is a "gender-specific expression. Consider replacing with *persons, human beings,* or *individuals.*"

The word *broad* used to set it off, too. Word 95's grammar checker objected to the use of *broad* in the following.

> He added that the Assistant Secretary of Defense for C3I is currently undertaking a Space Control Broad Area Review to examine the issues involved, which extend beyond the negation mission to include surveillance, protection, and prevention efforts.

"Sexist expression," scolded Word. "Avoid using this term to refer to women." Apparently it thought that "Space Control Broad" was a person.

Mindless avoidance of certain words will not help communication. Rather we need to examine the words we use to make sure they communicate what we want to say.

Parts of Sentences

Unless you have a good reason—and there are good reasons—you should write in complete sentences and edit fragments into complete sentences.

Mixtures of sentences and sentence fragments often show up in biographical summaries of employees in business proposals—things like "Jo graduated from Space Camp in 2001. Was first cadet to wear asteroid belt." It literally gives me a headache to read page after page of sentence fragments. Three little words would make that fragment into a sentence: "She was the first cadet to wear an asteroid belt." I think it's false economy to omit those words: It doesn't save much space, and it doesn't make the text easier to read. In short, it interferes with communication. One fragment I came across was "Schedule first to be sacrificed." It might have meant "The first one to produce a schedule will be cut from the team" (or maybe tossed into a volcano). Or it might have meant "Make your reservation now if you want to be sacrificed." Adding the missing words made the correct meaning clear: "The schedule is the first thing to be sacrificed."

Distinguishing Subjects, Predicates, and Objects

Writers who have trouble distinguishing subjects from objects tend to confuse *who* and *whom*, and *I* and *me*.

Who does something. Something happens to *whom*. "Who went with you?" (*Who* went; *who* did something.) "Whom did you see?" (*Whom* was seen; something happened to *whom*.)

Who and *whom* work in the same way as *he* and *him*, and hardly anybody mixes them up. You might write, "He went with you?" but not "Him went with you?" Likewise you might write, "Him did you see?" but not with the words in that order. Instead you would write, "Did you see him?" but not "Did you see he?" If you're not sure whether to use *who* or *whom*, think of *he* and *him*, and change the order of the words if necessary.

The same idea applies to *I* and *me*, but people often say things like "Marlene invited Steve and I to dinner."

Wrong! Cancel Steve's invitation and see what you have: "Marlene invited I to dinner." Right: "Marlene invited Steve and me to dinner."

Preposition Overkill

Trained by their grammar school teachers not to end a sentence with a preposition (the sort of nonsense up with which we should not put, Winston Churchill is supposed to have said), countless writers shy away from ever ending a sentence with a preposition, no matter how bad the result sounds.

Preposition and Article Underkill

Sentences lacking some articles or prepositions show up especially in biographical summaries in business proposals. "Jack authored report for WY/ME to address YU compatibility issues" (for example). It saves a tiny bit of space to leave out the article before *report*, but at a big cost in clarity: Did he write *a* report or *the* report? If he wrote the one and only report, that is more significant than writing one of many reports on the topic. "The grateful writers provided the editors donuts." The preposition *with* goes with *provide*; *provide* means "supply." If you supply donuts, fine. If you supply donuts to me, you need a preposition to say so. You don't supply me donuts or provide me donuts, you provide me with donuts. Even better is to reorder the sentence and use *to* instead of *with*: "The grateful writers provided donuts to the editors." This places the object right next to the verb—an improvement that often applies in editing.

Mistaken Junction[151]

Grammatically speaking, mistaken junction occurs when the reader links the wrong words, usually because the writer arranged them ambiguously. (These are all real quotations.)

> Extensive negotiation skills are need to meld the various maintenance activities into a solidified efficient repair scheme to ensure disruption to the Government Client are kept to a minimum.

"To ensure disruption" sounds like the task of the negotiator. The reader has to reach the end of the sentence before finding out that the object of *ensure* is a whole clause, not one word. Inserting *that* after *ensure* would have alerted the reader to the structure of the rest of the sentence: *ensure that disruption to the Government client is kept to a minimum.* (Yes, there are other things wrong with this sentence—*need* should be *needed*; *Client* should not be capitalized; *disruption* should be followed by *is*, not *are*—but I didn't make this one up.) Here's another:

> [A member of Congress] voiced concern that China is developing weapons using stolen U.S. warhead designs, and appears to be willing to sell this technology to rogue nations.

Who is willing to sell this technology to rogue nations? China? Or the Member of Congress? You could read it either way. Adding *that China* in front of *appears* would make the meaning unmistakable: "voiced concern that China is developing weapons using stolen U.S. warhead designs and that China appears to be willing to sell this technology to rogue nations."

And what will you find at the Treasury Department: information or exploited children?

> information related to ... exploited children at the U.S.
> Department of the Treasury

The reader might conclude that the Treasury Department violates child labor laws. Rewording it to say *the Treasury Department's information related to exploited children* would make it clear.

More funny business going on at the Treasury Department:

> The Secret Service conducts financial crimes and counterfeiting investigations

Until you get to the last word in the clause, you might think that the Secret Service conducts financial crimes. The same problem is evident here.

> The Miami Medical Examiner's Office receives a lot of their funding as a result of money laundering arrests and seizures

Mistaken junction can also occur when a sentence is finished on a following page. Suppose that, in the first example, "are kept to a minimum" had been on the next page. After reading about ensuring disruption, the reader might have gone back and forth between the two pages trying to figure out the meaning.

What would you make of these words at the end of a page?

> Execute Radiation Safety Officer

There was a key word at the end of it: *Execute Radiation Safety Officer responsibilities*. It would have been clearer (even if all the words were on one page) if written as *Execute the responsibilities of the Radiation Safety Officer*.

All the above examples are real, but I made this one up to illustrate another case of mistaken junction that occurs from the false economy of leaving out one word.

Dr. Jones works to ensure compliance, cohesion, categorization, and other tasks beginning with a *C* are accomplished.

Not till you get to the end of the sentence do you find out that everything following *to* was a clause; the sentence isn't saying that Dr. Jones works to ensure compliance, etc. (although she does); the sentence is saying she works to ensure *that* these things happen.

Avoid mistaken junction. Mistaken junction practically ensures disruption.

Misplaced Words

Only is probably the most commonly misplaced word. Try moving it around in this sentence and catch the changes in meaning: *Only I kicked him in the head.*

Nonrestrictive clauses are another example of commonly misplaced words: They tend to come loose and land in the wrong place also: *His theories concerned donuts, which were full of holes* gives a different meaning from *His theories, which were full of holes, concerned donuts.*

Sometimes the order of words makes comprehension difficult. Here's an example of too many words (twenty-one) between a verb (*put*) and adverb (*online*).

The U.S. Department of Transportation's Office of Hazardous Materials Safety has put their publication that offers a shortcut through layers of government that regulate the 800,000 daily hazardous shipments in the United States online.

You have to read a lot of words before you find out where the office put the publication. Also, *office* is singular, so it should have been *its publication*, not *their publication*. Here's an edited version.

The *2004 Emergency Response Guidebook* [the title of the guidebook was given elsewhere] published by the U.S. Department of Transportation's Office of Hazardous Materials Safety is now online. The publication offers a shortcut through layers of government that regulate the 800,000 daily hazardous shipments in the United States.

Here's a similar example, with thirty-three words between the subject (*using*) and the verb (*is*).

Using previous successes derived from containing contaminated food or meningitis epidemics as a basis for preparing for the devastating ramifications of a deliberately dispersed, virulent, and potentially lethal infectious agent by a thinking enemy is absurd.

And here's an edited version of it.

We must prepare for the devastating ramifications of a virulent and potentially lethal infectious agent deliberately dispersed by a thinking enemy. It is absurd to base our preparation on previous success in containing contaminated food or meningitis epidemics.

Punctuation

To thoroughly cover punctuation would take a whole book. *The Elements of Style* and *Words Into Type* both provide clear and, in the latter, comprehensive coverage of the topic, and each deserves a place on the desk of every editor. However, here I would like to mention a few points on which writers are continually tripping up—and therefore to which editors must be alert.

Commas

Commas have many purposes, and maybe whole books could be written just about commas. There are a few ways, however, in which they frequently are misused, misplaced, or omitted.

One common error is misplacement of commas typographically. In American usage, commas, like periods, always go inside quotation marks.

Wrong: "Have some more broccoli", she said.
Right: "Have some more broccoli," she said.

Even better: "Have some more chocolate-chip cookies," she said.

Commas are used to set off appositives and nonrestrictive clauses and phrases. (See the discussion of *which* and *that* in chapter seven.)

An appositive names the same thing as what went before. In "Boston, the largest city in Massachusetts, was our home," *the largest city in Massachusetts* is an appositive. *Boston* and *the largest city in Massachusetts* mean the same thing: "Boston was our home" means the same thing as "The largest city in Massachusetts was our home." But "Florida is a hamlet in the Berkshire Mountains of Massachusetts" is not an appositive. Florida is a hamlet, but a hamlet in the Berkshire Mountains of Massachusetts isn't necessarily Florida.

A nonrestrictive or nonessential clause or phrase gives information that could be left out without changing the meaning.

In "Oak trees without leaves give no shade," *without leaves* is restrictive or essential information. In "Oak trees, without leaves, give no shade," the commas around *without leaves* tell the reader that those two words give nonessential information, but that isn't true: "Oak trees give no shade" has a very different meaning.

In "Oak trees, which grow from acorns, can be fifty feet tall," *which grow from acorns* is extra, nonessential information. Leave it out, and the sentence has the same basic meaning: "Oak trees can be fifty feet tall."

It is worth noting that a state name following a city name is set off by two commas, not one: "We lived in Boston, Massachusetts, until 1979"; not "We lived in Boston, Massachusetts until 1979." In that sentence, *Massachusetts* is nonrestrictive, giving additional but nonessential information, and is set off by commas. Leaving out a comma can cause what EEI (formerly Editorial Experts Inc.) calls a squinting modifier, as in this example: "After a tornado flattened nearly all of Greensburg, Kan. Guard shortfalls delayed the state's emergency response." Does *Kan.* go with *Greensburg* or *Guard*? It could go with either, because the Kansas Guard responded in Greensburg, Kansas. But it can't go with both, so you have to pick one.

The same rule applies to references to a month, date, and year. The year is additional information, although if you're referring to any year but the current one you'll want to include it.

> **Wrong:** "On April 17, 1970 Apollo 13 returned to earth."
> **Right:** "On April 17, 1970, Apollo 13 returned to earth."

Commas are also used to set off items in a series. A rule of thumb is that a comma should be inserted where the word *and* could be used: "The colorful, bright Christmas lights decorated the window." The lights were colorful *and* bright, so a comma is correct between those words. The lights were not "bright and Christmas," so a comma between those words would be wrong.

When a series ends with a conjunction, the comma before the conjunction (known as the "serial comma") is optional, unless the meaning would be unclear without it. Whether to use a serial comma all the time is up to the individual publisher.

"The three principal types of rock are sedimentary, igneous, and metamorphic" would be clear without the comma after *igneous*.

Commas in direct address separate the name of the one being addressed. It should be "Good morning, America," not "Good morning America," although when referring to the TV show we need to use its actual name, however badly punctuated it is.

Language columnist William Safire included some comments on commas in his book *Take My Word for It*.[152]

> "Where have all the commas gone?" writes Gilbert Cranberg, former editorial writer of *The Des Moines Register*. "... Commas are free. Why don't they use them?" ...
>
> "I should not give away commas as generously as Gilbert Cranberg does [wrote Elizabeth Chapman Hewitt of Lincoln, Mass.] ... Commas after restrictive clauses are expensive. What is one to make of: 'People, who live in glass houses, shouldn't throw stones'?"

Hyphens[153]

Editors spend countless hours inserting hyphens when we could be doing better things if only more writers grasped the simple principles involved. Hyphens are used to link words that belong together but might be misread without the hyphen. Hyphens explain things. Hyphens prevent misunderstanding. As I have told students in editing classes, hyphens are our friends.

Sometimes the context indicates which words go together even without punctuation to help the reader. "He handed me a ten dollar bill" would be clear without the grammatically correct hyphen in *ten-dollar*, but "He paid me with ten dollar bills" is unclear. Did he pay me ten dollars in singles or a much greater amount in tens? That's why number-noun combinations are hyphenated. Like some other grammatical constructions, they are so prone to misreading without hyphens that it is standard practice to use hyphens in every instance. A look at the following examples will show how the absence of hyphens can spread confusion.

Number-adjective combinations generally need hyphens. If "forty odd people attended the conference," does that mean forty weird people? A hyphen in "forty-odd" indicates that those two words go together.

> **Unclear:** "Move the five gallon containers of lemonade." (Are there five one-gallon containers or an undetermined number of five-gallon containers?)
> **Clear:** "Move the five-gallon containers of lemonade."

Adjective-noun combinations usually need hyphens, too. "High power lines" may be strung from towers. "High-power lines" carry heavy voltage, even if the lines are buried.

> **Unclear:** "I need a hot water bottle." (A water bottle that is hot or a bottle designed to hold hot water?)
> **Clear:** "I need a hot-water bottle."

Verb-adverb combinations usually need hyphens. If someone is the "best known artist," maybe there are better artists who are unknown. *Best* could refer to *known* or *artist*. A hyphen between those words tells the reader that this artist is the most famous. (Adverbs ending in -*ly* don't need a hyphen, since they can't combine with anything except the verb. "A barely known artist" doesn't need a hyphen.)

> **Unclear:** "She wore a buttoned down coat." (A down coat buttoned or a coat buttoned securely?)
> **Clear:** "She wore a buttoned-down coat."

> **Clear without a hyphen:** "These are frequently made errors."

Combinations of two adjectives need hyphens. If "it came with an extra long handle," did it have a spare long handle or an especially long handle? "Extra-long handle" is unambiguous.

Noun-participle combinations need hyphens.

> **Unclear:** "I saw a man eating shark." (A man eating shark meat or a shark that eats men?)
> **Clear:** "I saw a man-eating shark."

> **Unclear:** "I ate a hard boiled egg." (A hard egg?)
> **Clear:** "I ate a hard-boiled egg."

Finally, if the combination comes at the end of a phrase or sentence, a hyphen may be unnecessary. "The handle was extra long" is clear. Just remember the hyphen's purpose: Whenever the meaning could be unclear, a hyphen shows the reader that certain words go together.

Dashes[154]

Dashes are everywhere—though sometimes not where they belong, and often under strength: that is, an en dash where the longer em dash is called for, or a mere hyphen where an en dash is needed. The two most common dashes are the em dash and the en dash, so called because they are the width of a capital *M* and a capital *N*, respectively: — and –. Em dashes are used for separating groups of words—especially words that could be set off by parentheses—and therefore em dashes often show up in pairs. In typewriting, a pair of hyphens substitutes for an em dash.

Hyphens join words; em dashes separate them. En dashes do both, as in "the New York–Chicago *Lake Shore Limited*": "New York–Chicago" is a modifying phrase, so *New York* and *Chicago* need to be joined, but, visually, a hyphen joins the wrong elements, putting *York* and *Chicago* closer together than *New* and *York*: "New York-Chicago" (although the Associated Press and Government Printing Office styles don't use en dashes and would have it as "New York-Chicago"). "Boston-Chicago" would look fine with a hyphen, but joining a pair of words to a single word or to another pair requires an en dash.

En dashes have risen from obscurity. They have been pressed into service where their big brothers always reigned, frequently with spaces to help them shoulder aside the words they're not quite strong enough to separate.

Instead of "Use em dashes—they're stronger," you might see "Use en dashes–they're smaller and must be cheaper." As you can see, that en dash isn't big enough to visually separate two independent clauses. You might see an attempt to compensate in the form of "Use en dashes plus spaces – en dashes are probably cheaper, and the spaces are free."

Although whether to add spaces around em dashes is a matter of typographical style — some major publishers do so — in practice it can cause problems. Programs such as Microsoft Word and InDesign are set up to keep an em dash with the preceding word when the dash falls at the end of a line. Because an em dash represents a major break in a sentence, it's polite to let the reader know right away rather than wait till the beginning of the next line. If the dash is preceded by a space, however, the aforementioned programs will let the dash slip to the next line. You could use nonbreaking spaces, but doing so creates extra work. *Words Into Type* has an excellent discussion of dashes and their uses.

Suspended Modifiers

When a combination of three words is made up of two separated words joined to a third, they form a suspended modifier.

Example: "Tip editors with ten- and twenty-dollar bills." The *ten* and *twenty* combine with *dollar*, but, according to Newton's laws, cannot be in the same place at the same time. So one is suspended, or left hanging. The hyphen indicates that it combines with something else; the space after the hyphen indicates that the word doesn't combine with the very next word.

In *Against the Grain* magazine, in an article by Randy Engel called "Why the Population Council Is a Rockefeller Baby" (see chapter four if you want to know why), there's a reference to "St. Louis' KETC-TV educational television station's 12-15 minute TV programs." This is a good example of a suspended modifier that isn't punctuated clearly. It could suggest a dozen or more programs each one minute in length, such as public-service announcements, in which case it should read, "12 to 15 one-minute TV programs"; if there are many programs twelve to fifteen minutes in length, it should read, "12- to 15-minute TV programs." By the way, in that phrase "TV" is redundant: we've already been told that it's a TV station, so what other kind of program would KETC be airing?

Parentheses and Brackets[155]

A parenthesis is a digression or interlude, according to *Merriam-Webster's Collegiate Dictionary*, 10th edition. Digressions are separated from the rest of a sentence by a pair of parentheses or, in some cases, by brackets. The digression might be a single word (parenthetically), a phrase (such as an explanation), numbers or letters (for example, *1, 2, 3* ...), or even an entire sentence.

If a digression occurs within parentheses, brackets are used. Parentheses should not appear within parentheses except in special cases, such as some mathematical expressions or legal citations. (Brackets within parentheses can look awkward [creating a second level of parenthesis], and *Words Into Type* recommends using em dashes in place of brackets where possible.)

Brackets are also used to indicate anything added to a quotation. "The matter enclosed [in brackets] may be wholly independent of the text, or it may be words supplied to secure complete and understandable sentences," notes *Words Into Type*.[156] In any case, it is important to distinguish anything that is not part of the quotation. Some styles, such as that used by the Associated Press, do not use brackets (using only parentheses) and are the poorer for it, because the lack of brackets makes it hard to distinguish a speaker's or writer's parenthetical remarks from words added by a reporter or editor.

Parentheses often contain (though they are not designed to hold) isolated sentence fragments (I'll give an example shortly). Few things look so lonely as isolated sentence fragments. Wrapping them up in parentheses doesn't solve the problem, either. They look like a baby in a basket left hopefully on a doorstep. (poor baby) That's an example of an abandoned fragment—it follows the sentence (meaning it comes after the period) but has no punctuation or capitalization of its own. In that case the best solution is to open the door and bring the fragment inside the sentence (much better). Now the phrase in parentheses is before the period, so it doesn't need additional punctuation or capitalization.

Usually these abandoned fragments take the form of a cross-reference or citation: (figure 2) or (Dunham, 2012). The rule still applies. Sentences get the first word capped and take a period, question mark, or exclamation point at the end. Fragments don't.

See figure 2 (instead of just *figure 2*) is an example of a complete sentence, however. It could be placed in parentheses within another sentence, with the word *see* lowercase (see figure 2), or *See figure 2* could be a sentence by itself and still be set off by parentheses: (See figure 2.).

To put it another way, treat sentences as sentences and fragments as fragments, whether or not they're enclosed in parentheses. But have a heart—bring those poor fragments inside a sentence. Don't leave them out on the doorstep.

Slashes[157]

The most abused punctuation mark? For my money (paltry though that may be), it's the slash. According to *Words Into Type*, the slash has a few standard uses: in fractions, or as a sign for shillings, or to indicate line breaks in bibliographical matter or poetry. Also, "between *and* and *or* it means 'or.'"[158]

In the hands of many technical writers, however, the slash is treated like a utility conjunction. Here is an example from an Air Force document, *New World Vistas*.

> Information and Space will become inextricably entwined. The Information/ Space milieu will interact strongly with the air and ground components ...

What does that slash signify? Clearly this is not poetry (though that space after the slash might suggest it), nor are *Information* and *Space* numerator and denominator. Nor could the slash mean "or"—the milieu involves information *and* space, "inextricably entwined." The slash seems to mean *and*, or maybe *plus*, or *combined with*.

Another example from that same document: "human/machine interface." Again the slash seems to indicate not alternatives but a joining or meeting. Ordinarily a hyphen would be used: *human-machine interface*.

A slash, wrote Richard Mitchell in *The Graves of Academe*, "reveals that no one has paid any thoughtful attention to the conjunction, and thus to the *exact* nature of the relationship."[159]

Apostrophes

Besides their straightforward role of marking omitted letters in contractions, apostrophes have two uses that cause confusion: forming possessives and forming plurals.

Singular nouns usually have their possessive formed by addition of *'s*: *the governor's budget, the newspaper's publisher, fielder's choice*. Plural nouns that don't end in *s* also form the possessive by the addition of *'s*: *children's books, the geese's honking, alumni's addresses*. Plural nouns get just an apostrophe if they end in *s*: *states' rights, two weeks' vacation, bells' ringing*. Whether to add *'s* or only an apostrophe to words that already end in an *s* sound is a matter of preference. A common rule is to add the *'s* only if it is pronounced—*the bus's wheels, the tortoise's shell*—as opposed to *Jesus' mother, old times' sake*. The glaring exception to the use of apostrophes to form possessives concerns pronouns, which for some reason never get apostrophes: *his, hers, ours, its, theirs, yours*.

Although plurals are usually formed by adding an *s* or by changing the spelling (*goose* to *geese*, *child* to *children*), apostrophes are sometimes used to form plurals that would be hard to read if only an *s* were added— particularly single letters. "There are three is in *initiate*" requires at least two glances to decipher. "There are three i's in *initiate*" should be clear at first glance. This modest and rare use of apostrophes to form plurals is abused with insertion of apostrophes in all sorts of places where they don't belong, especially proper names. My family is the Dunhams, not the Dunham's. If one of us were famous, then that person might claim to be "*the* Dunham" and take possession of all that is the Dunham's. I saw this business of inserting apostrophes carried to its ultimate (at least I hope it goes no further) on the back of a pickup truck.

PWR-washing
- Deck's
- Fence's
- Home's

At least that example exhibits parallel construction: Each item in the list logically follows the word *washing*.

Here's an example of ridiculously skewed construction—only the first item logically follows the word *provides*.

Photo copyright Steve Dunham, 2013.

Ellipsis Points[160]

Ellipsis points (…) indicate something left out.

"Terminal punctuation is retained before points of ellipsis," explains *Words Into Type*.[161] If the omission comes after a sentence, include whatever ended the sentence: period, question mark, or exclamation point. Suppose we want to abridge Garrison Keillor's fantasy that his family were really Italians, taken from *Lake Wobegon Days*.

> We weren't who we thought we were, we were the Keillorinis! Presto! Prestone! My father rushed to the closet and hauled out giant oil paintings of fat ladies, statues of saints, bottles of wine, and in rushed the relatives, hollering and carrying platters of spicy spaghetti, and my father would turn to me and say, "Eduardo! Eduardo, my son!" and throw his arms around me and plant big wet smackers on my cheeks.

If we cut *Presto! Prestone!* and everything after *spaghetti* and insert ellipsis points, we get this.

> We weren't who we thought we were, we were the Keillorinis! … My father rushed to the closet and hauled out giant oil paintings of fat ladies, statues of saints, bottles of wine, and in rushed the relatives, hollering and carrying platters of spicy spaghetti …

We keep the exclamation point after *Keillorinis* because it ends the sentence, but the quotation ends with ellipsis points and no period because we left off in the middle of a sentence. *Words Into Type* notes that "points of ellipsis are usually unnecessary at the beginning or the end of a quotation,"[162] explaining that it is ordinarily not necessary to emphasize that a quotation has been excerpted from a larger whole. Other punctuation at the end of a quotation may be included if it aids clarity. Finally, "An omission of whole paragraphs or stanzas of poetry, a change of subject, or the lapse of time may be indicated by a line of points or a line of asterisks."[163]

Colons and Semicolons[164]

Both the colon (:) and the semicolon (;) are used to separate independent clauses—groups of words that could stand on their own as sentences. Maybe that's why these two punctuation marks get confused so often. People even get the names mixed up. Remember that *semi* means "half"; the colon is all one thing (dots), and the semicolon is half comma and half dot.

Colons are often used to introduce lists, but only if the colon follows a complete sentence. "I like dessert: cakes, pies, cookies, ice cream—anything sweet." But "I like dessert, such as" is not a complete sentence, so there should be no colon in the following: "I like dessert, such as: cakes, pies, cookies, ice cream—anything sweet."

Nor should a colon separate a verb from its object. "I like: dessert" is wrong. Adding a long list after *dessert* wouldn't make the colon right, nor would it be the best way to present the information.

Colons are also used after formal salutations in a letter (such as "Dear friend of the cows:"); other uses for colons are to separate hours from minutes ("Let's stop work at 3:30 today"), chapter from verse in scripture citations ("Luke 12:18"), numerals in a ratio ("2:1"), or city from publisher in a bibliographical citation ("Boston: Little, Brown").

Colons may be used to join two clauses or sentences when one follows from the other. "She wouldn't eat the cake: She's allergic to chocolate." That's where the duties of colons overlap with those of semicolons. That sentence could have a semicolon instead; the colon is a slightly better choice because it indicates that the thoughts are not just parallel but closely related. Separating independent clauses is the main job of semicolons. Their other job is to separate groups that have items separated by commas, such as lists of cities and states. The following series is hard to understand with only commas: "West New York, N.J., New York, N.Y., and East New York, N.Y., are within twenty miles of one another." Semicolons break up the units that are themselves divided by commas: "West New York, N.J.; New York, N.Y.; and East New York, N.Y.; are within twenty miles of one another."

Finally, colons and semicolons next to quotation marks and parentheses go outside those punctuation marks. *We heard them perform last night (in a recital): He played "Moonlight Sonata"; she performed "Rhapsody in Blue."*

Unorthodox but Acceptable Punctuation

Vince Lombardi was quoted as saying, "You don't do things right once in a while, you do them right all the time." In *Let a Simile Be Your Umbrella*, William Safire wrote:

> I say that sentence contains two independent clauses requiring a semicolon; as it stands, the sentence is joined into a "comma splice" … Sol Steinmetz, the Hall of Fame lexicographer, disagrees: "Because the emphasis here is on 'once in a while,' a semicolon doesn't fit because it would separate a continuous thought into two ideas. The sentence is punctuated correctly with a comma because there is a parallel between the two independent clauses."[165]

Style

Style is a way of doing things. In publishing it can refer to a writer's style—formal, for example, or breezy. It also refers to a system of standardization. Style makes it easier for editors to achieve consistency. It establishes one way of doing things when more than one correct choice exists. It is correct to spell out all numbers less than 100. It is also correct to spell out only numbers less than 10. Rather than have to choose one way or the other with every publication, style defines one way of doing things.

Should commas be used before the conjunction in a series of words? Should *traveling* be spelled with one *l* or two? Should *Congressional* always be capitalized? Should *state* be capitalized in the phrase *Washington state*? Are personal pronouns capitalized when they refer to

God?* A style guide answers such questions so that they do not need to be answered again and again.

If *fifteen* is spelled out in some publications and not in others, then an extra degree of alertness is required to remember which style applies to the publication in question. When editors and proofreaders are used to seeing things done a certain way, an alarm bell will go off in their heads when they see something different.

The style established by the University of Chicago Press is particularly suited to academic books. Associated Press style has been developed and refined to suit the needs of newspapers, and it is used by magazines as well.

What House Style Is and Why It Exists

House style establishes the publisher's way of doing things. Although style guides attempt to be comprehensive, frequently questions will arise that are not specifically addressed in the guide, and publishers often find some aspects of a style guide unsuited to their publications. House style, therefore, often is defined as following an existing style guide, such as *The Associated Press Stylebook*, plus any exceptions to that guide. Sometimes a publisher will use two different styles—Associated Press style for press releases, for example, and maybe the American Psychological Association style for scientific books.

Major news sources, such as *The New York Times* and the British Broadcasting Corporation, publish their own style guides, and you can find style guides designed for a specific industry or other audience as well: The American Medical Association, the American Chemical Association, the Council of Science Editors, and the Modern Language Association of America all publish style guides, and for business writing you might want to use *The Gregg Reference Manual* or the *Franklin Covey Style Guide*.

Proper names, titles, and other words peculiar to an organization often are listed in the style guide, along with peculiarities of usage, such

---

*   If the author is frequently quoting a particular version of the Bible, a good
     solution is to follow the capitalization style in that version.

as whether to use the pronoun *it* to describe babies (the usage is long established, as in "It's a boy!"), and whether to rewrite sentences in the plural to avoid the often objectionable *he* and *his* for anonymous persons (as in changing "every editor met his deadline" to "all the editors met their deadlines") and avoid the clumsy construction *his or her*. (See "His 'n' Her Pronouns.")

All these things are matters of style. "It's not a matter of being correct or incorrect. It's only a style," wrote Carol Fisher Saller, host of the Subversive Copy Editor blog.[166]

"Treatises like *Chicago* are merely suggestions, guides, if you will, to a method that enhances clarity and consistency," wrote Rich Adin on his blog, An American Editor.[167]

"The important thing is not that you use any one style over another," said editor Dave Fessenden, "but that for any particular piece you edit, you choose one style and stick with it, for the sake of consistency."

6

Typography

An editor might have no responsibility for the appearance of the typeset words, but the proofreader does, and very often the editor and proof-reader are the same person. Although the choice of font, margins, and type size affect readability (and hence communication), the editor and proofreader are probably not involved in those choices unless they are doing layout and design work, too, as sometimes happens.

Once the words are typeset, however, some rules apply for clear communication. Two of them involve word breaks and line breaks.

Breaking Words

Words Into Type offers some general rules about breaking words at the end of a line (first of all, follow a dictionary):[168] "A word may be divided only at the end of a syllable." Division between double conso-nants is preferable unless the pair is part of the root word, as in *tollbooth*. Dividing before a consonant is better than dividing before a vowel. Endings such as *-tion* and *-tial* should not be split. Compound words that contain a hyphen (such as *self-interest*) should be split only at the existing hyphen. And words should not be split across nonfacing pages. *Words Into Type* has some more to say about how to divide words, but those are the salient points.

Keeping Certain Words Together

The end of a line and the end of a page force the reader to pause, however slightly. These pauses can cause confusion. In "Keeping Things Together,"[169] editor Julie Wright wrote:

> This problem becomes most apparent when measurements are expressed in groups of numbers and words, as in *3 years* or *$25 million*. Ending one line with *3* and beginning the next with *years* causes a gap in thought when readers must ask, "3 what?" When a line ends with *$25* and the next begins with *million*, readers first register one amount in their minds, then take a split second to amend it. Dates are another example of number and word groups that should stay together. If a date (for example, September 5, 1999), must be divided, it is better to divide it before the year rather than between the month and the day. …
>
> Dividing names can also make reading more difficult. This may be hard to avoid with a series of names, but here are a few guidelines: (1) Always keep titles with the name. This goes for titles that precede the name (Dr., Mr., or Gen.) as well as those that follow it (Ph.D. or III). (2) Where there is a middle name or initial, it should go with the first name. (3) Don't separate last names of more than one word (Van Buren or Saint James).
>
> Poorly split headings may qualify as ridiculous if not disastrous. An actual package in a supermarket was labeled

100% Fat

Free Meatballs

> "Fat-free" should have been joined by a hyphen anyway, but putting the words on different lines aggravates the offense and could give shoppers a wrong idea of the contents. The same problem was writ large on an outdoor sign:

ENJOY THE HASSLE

FREE OIL CHANGE

Some phrases require more than careful line division. One sentence that came across our editorial desk referred to "proper execution of next of kin notification." This phrase is liable to shock readers until they reach the last word. In such a case, the best solution is to rewrite the sentence—for instance, "proper notification of next of kin."

Keep in mind, too, how things may look after they are typeset. If *Do you believe your boss would consent?* comes near a page break, the last words on the page might be *Do you believe your boss*, giving the reader a wrong idea of how the sentence will end.

Think of a line break or a page break as a pause: will the sentence continue in the same apparent direction, or will the reader get a surprise ending?

Type and Layout

An editor may well be involved in typography and layout, in which case it helps to acquire some basic knowledge about type and design.

Although the section on typography in *Words Into Type* is out of date in its descriptions of how type is set, the concepts of good typography are mostly the same. The "Choice of Size and Face" section has helpful information on, for example, standards of type sizes for adults and children.

To learn the essentials of design, I think you can't do better than the books by Robin Williams (not the famous comedian but still an entertaining and informative writer). She emphasizes four principles: proximity, repetition, alignment, and contrast. Her books—including *The Non-Designer's Design Book*,[170] *The Non-Designer's Type Book*,[171] and *The Non-Designer's Web Book*[172]—will help an editor work better with artists, designers, and typographers, and they will even help you make sensible, if not necessarily artistic, layout decisions.

One thing I tell authors is "Don't try to do the layout for the publisher." Authors tend to be fond of embellishing manuscripts with decorative fonts, pictures with text wrapping around them, centered headings, and other typographical bling. All of that will probably be lost.

The book designer will most likely use a layout program rather than a word-processing program to make up the pages for a book or other publication and will do so with a trained professional eye. As long as the elements of a manuscript are legible and clearly distinguished (marking, for example, the heading levels—H1, H2, and H3 are standard notations for three levels of headings), the author should not try to make the manuscript prettier.

"There are exceptions," noted editor Dave Fessenden. "Some poets will write a poem that *has* to be typeset to a particular shape on the page. An author may have an accompanying chart that makes no sense if the explanatory paragraph is not next to it." In such cases, the author should provide instructions to the editor explaining what is necessary. The instructions are important, because a poem that has been physically arranged with an assortment of tabs, returns, and spaces might lose some or all of those things going from a word-processing program to a layout program.

◼◼ Text Boxes Are Evil

Of all the things that are wrong about [Microsoft] Word, the text (and graphic) boxes are the absolute worst. Text boxes don't stick in place; text boxes do not break over pages; if the text box is too big for the page or not big enough to display all of the text it holds, it gives no clue that there is hidden [text within the box]; text boxes obscure text and other text and graphic boxes—basically, text boxes are evil and not easy to get rid of. Need to box some text? Use a table cell. It works just as well and has none of the evil features of a text box.

—Rich Adin on his blog, An American Editor[173]

Another evil of the text box: Authors often put critical pieces of text in them, but when transferred to a layout program (or sometimes, even when transferred to the editor in the same word-processing program) the boxes disappear, and that text is *gone*!

—Editor Dave Fessenden

7

A Few Tips

The rules of grammar, punctuation, and usage are thoroughly spelled out in sources such as *The Elements of Style* and *Words Into Type*. I particularly like the clear examples given in *Words Into Type*. Both of those books also have helpful lists of misused words. Even if you have those books, there are some writing and editing problems that arise so often that I think it's worth discussing a few of them here.

Misused Words

Comprised and Composed

"'Comprised of' is always wrong …" wrote copy editor Laura Moyer. "'Comprise' is a perfectly useful word. It means to encompass …"[174] She quoted *The Associated Press Stylebook*'s examples of how to use the word *comprise* correctly.

> "The United States comprises 50 states. The jury comprises five men and seven women. The zoo comprises many animals."
> … So if we're not using "comprised of," what should we use?
> "Comprises" usually works.
> But sometimes what you want is the phrase "composed of."[175]

Three Hands Full

Another puzzle for writers and editors concerns plurals of *-fuls*. Does *handful* become *hands full* or *handfuls*? If the *-ful* is a measure of something, and you have more than one of it, then you have a plural *-ful—handfuls*.

Three cupfuls is 24 ounces liquid measure, even if it's in 6 cups half full. "Three cups full" means three actual cups, all full.

That and Which

Two words that are often misused are *that* and *which*. Although the word *which* in restrictive (or "essential") clauses has long-established usage, it also can create confusion, especially if the punctuation is incorrect or inadvertently dropped.

For this reason, the school of thought among most editors today seems to be that *which* should be used only in nonrestrictive (or "nonessential") clauses.

A restrictive clause changes the meaning of the sentence; a nonrestrictive clause can be deleted without affecting the meaning. In the sentence "The flavor of ice cream that I like least is broccoli," the words *that I like least* are a restrictive clause. Without them, the sentence would read "The flavor of ice cream is broccoli," and would have a different meaning.

In the sentence "Broccoli ice cream, which tastes horrible, is the flavor I like least," the words *which tastes horrible* are a nonrestrictive clause. Without them, the sentence would read, "Broccoli ice cream is the flavor I like least." The meaning would be the same; the nonrestrictive clause merely gives more information.

It would not be wholly incorrect to write, "The flavor of ice cream which I like least is broccoli." Confusion arises if the reader sees *which* and supposes that commas were accidentally left out and that a nonrestrictive clause was intended: "The flavor of ice cream, which I like least, is broccoli." The meaning then would seem to be "The flavor being served is broccoli, and that's the flavor I like least."

Likewise, when commas do get left out, the meaning is again distorted: "Broccoli ice cream which tastes horrible is the flavor I like least" now seems to say, "I dislike only broccoli ice cream that tastes horrible; some broccoli ice cream does not."

The above sentences indicate, in somewhat repulsive fashion, the reason for the school of thought that assigns *that* to restrictive clauses and *which* to nonrestrictive. In restrictive clauses, sometimes the word *that* can be omitted, as in "Broccoli ice cream is the flavor [that] I like least."

Appositives are a particular type of nonrestrictive phrase, or often just a single word—they identify or are equal to the word in question. Appositives are always set off by commas. "Our cat, Fluffy, has downy fur." (*Our cat* = *Fluffy* if we have only one cat. Then the sentence would have the same meaning if either *Our cat* or *Fluffy* were taken out.)

Strange Traditions[176]

In America we have some strange traditions—infectious diseases, for example. The National Center for Infectious Diseases "is committed to the prevention and control of traditional, new and reemerging infectious diseases."

How about the traditions of "friction, uncertainty, fluidity, and disorder," "terrorist incidents," or "facilities or equipment"? I've seen all these labeled "traditional." Some other traditions are "fan blade-out and oil starvation testing," planning templates, database environments, cockpit instruments, and microorganisms that cause anthrax, Q fever, and dengue.

In the good old days we had pleasanter traditions: Thanksgiving dinners, vacations at the seashore, going to the fireworks on the Fourth of July. Even the sad traditions, such as getting together with family after a funeral, were not as impersonal as facilities or equipment, nor as antisocial as terrorist incidents.

Will today's children some day look back with fondness on the traditions of oil starvation testing and database environments? Or is the word *traditional* being sorely abused?

William Safire, in *Take My Word for It*,[177] noted that the words "*usual* (common or frequent occurrence) ... *customary* (conventional, or conforming to previous practice), *habitual* (unfailing repetition), and *typical* (following a pattern)" all have similar meanings but are still different.

However, "*traditional*, which used to mean 'time-honored,' … is undergoing a vogue use to mean just about everything in the paragraph above. …

"When in doubt remember Claude Rains in *Casablanca*: He did not say, 'Round up the traditional suspects.'"[178]

Formerly[179]

We wouldn't write, "Former President Lincoln authored the Emancipation Proclamation," or, "Former President Nixon resigned." They did those things as president. Former President Nixon wrote his memoirs—after he wasn't president any more.

Former indicates what something or somebody used to be, but it speaks of a more recent status. In describing events of the past, however, tell it the way it was.

"The former Soviet Union had to go through the same transformation in the '60s, after the Cuban Missile Crisis," said Captain Doug Littlejohns, Royal Navy, in an interview in Tom Clancy's book *SSN*.[180] No, that was the Soviet Union. The *former* Soviet Union is Russia and the other states that used to be the USSR.

Homophones and Other Words That Get Mixed Up[181]

"Tuesday's ½ Price Burgers," said the sign in a restaurant window in Alexandria, Virginia. It was a Monday when I spotted the sign, and I wondered whether the next day's burgers were being sold cheaply ahead of time, sort of like a prepublication discount, or whether they were six days old. Actually, I knew that the restaurateur had mixed up *Tuesdays* and *Tuesday's*, and that the sign really meant that a customer could buy a half-price burger on Tuesdays. A little more punctuation would have helped, too. A spell-checker would not.

A spell-checker merely compares the words in a document against a list. If there's a match, it goes on to the next word. It doesn't know whether you used the *right* word (although Microsoft Word has gotten better at spotting some errors and suggesting alternatives). That's why you might read about "the Service Life Enchantment Program" (it works like magic, but *Enchantment* should have been *Enhancement*) or the "Ad Hoc Space Lunch study" (can we do lunch tomorrow on the International Space Station?), "as demonstrated in Dessert Storm" (that was one awful food fight!).

All these phrases appeared (before editing) in work written by a "team of over 650 processionals" (the company's parade of talent). None of these errors would be caught by a spell-checker. The fact is, all a spell-check can do is guarantee that your mistakes are spelled correctly.

One way to catch such mistakes is to make a list of mistyped words that appear often in your documents and then search for them before printing a file or publishing it. I call this my list of bad words. *Asses* is a bad word. So are *posses*, *mange*, *polices*, and *theses*. They are bad because they almost never are used on purpose in company documents, but they turn up far too often and are easy to overlook. They are mistyped versions of *assess*, *possess*, *manage*, *policies*, and *these*. It's easy to read them and not notice that they're wrong. I once edited an article about public health and didn't notice until I searched for bad words that *public* appeared as *pubic* in five places. One of my favorite typos, which I made into a cookie jar label, was *bio-warfare treats* (instead of *threats*). Searching for bad words takes only a minute and can save you from making embarrassing mistakes. I've seen *asses* instead of *assess* in a 24-point headline. The U.S. Attorneys' Criminal Resource Manual online has a section headlined "Federal Explosive Statues."

Sometimes the wrong word works its way in, turning positives into negatives. One system was to be built on "globally inoperable infrastructure and services" (the writer meant *interoperable*). One committee's "goal was to develop specific, actionable recommendations" (*actionable* can mean "giving grounds for a lawsuit"*). This would be admirable honesty if they were really building a system out of things that don't work and then suggesting that the client sue them.

---

* Although it has developed a quite different positive meaning, too, but the reader may not know which meaning was intended—see the section on Janus words.

Errors involving homophones (words spelled differently that sound the same) seem to be increasingly common, perhaps because writers rely too much on spell-checking software, which usually won't spot a homophone error as long as the word appears on the dictionary list. (See chapter nine for a few more words about spell-checkers.)

"Much of the credit for diffusing this incorrect information must go to …" stated *The Home School Court Report* newsletter. *To diffuse* means "to spread out" or "to disseminate." Surely the writer did not mean to give credit for spreading misinformation. *To defuse* means "to render harmless," as in removing the fuse from a bomb. The writer probably meant that credit should go to the people who, by countering incorrect information, defused an explosive situation. *Diffuse* and *defuse* are not quite homophones—the long *e* in *defuse* is normally pronounced—but they are close enough to confuse an otherwise literate writer.

With otherwise literate writers tripping up, editors must constantly be on guard for homophone errors. The confusion of *your* and *you're*, or *its* and *it's*, will usually produce a glaring error. (A rule of thumb: possessive pronouns ending in *s—its, ours,* and *hers,* for example—do not use an apostrophe.) Other homophones, such as *hoard* and *horde,* or *allusive* and *elusive,* can easily slip past an inattentive editor.

I once caught an author calling a jalousie window a "jealousy window"; maybe you watch the Joneses through a jealousy window.

I spotted *damn* instead of *dam* in *The Killer Angels* by Michael Shaara: "as water builds behind a damn" (on page 204 in the Ballantine paperback edition), when the book was in its twenty-fifth printing—which brings us obliquely to correction files. For any publication that is going to be reprinted, the publisher should keep a file of corrections to be made on future printings. If there is no time or budget for someone in-house to read the longer publications again before they are reprinted, then the publisher must depend on alert readers who kindly point out errors to the publisher.

It helps if an editor enjoys browsing in a dictionary now and then, and often takes the time to look up words to be sure of their meaning.

Theodore Bernstein's book *The Careful Writer* is a valuable resource for editors; it points out many common errors in word usage. Occasional perusal of the book will help an editor remain attuned to the differences between frequently confused words and aware of the nuances in meaning.

Acronym Soup[182]

"This chart shows that we have a lot of acronyms," I heard a speaker say, poking fun at his own slide. If nothing else, the chart did show that. The slide he was projecting consisted principally of capital letters in boxes connected by lines and arrows.

Like other words, acronyms (which are not just initials, but abbreviations pronounced as if they were words) have a purpose: communication. They can be a faster, more concise form of transmitting ideas. As a kind of verbal shorthand, they can make reference to concepts known to both writer and reader.

Sometimes an acronym becomes so popularly known that it persists long after the words it stands for have disappeared—*UNICEF*, for example, once stood for "United Nations International Children's Emergency Fund." Even though the organization's name has changed to "United Nations Children's Fund," the acronym *UNICEF* remains the official abbreviation. When you have achieved positive name recognition among the public, you probably don't want to change the name by which you're known.

Sometimes the shortened form of an abbreviation becomes better known than the original words: "radio detection and ranging," "North Atlantic Treaty Organization," and "light amplification by stimulated emission of radiation" are better known as *radar*, *NATO*, and *laser*.

■■ What Is an Acronym?

UNICEF, like *radar*, is an acronym—an abbreviation that is pronounced as a word, not just by saying the letters. *TNT* and *DNA* are not acronyms: We pronounce them "T-N-T" and

> "D-N-A," not "tint" and "deena." As William Safire noted in *Watching My Language*, "'AIDS' is the best-known acronym … being replaced by 'H.I.V.' infection—not an acronym, with the letters pronounced individually."[183]

Everybody Knows This …

Acronyms and other abbreviations may be used like ordinary words when their meaning is known to both writer and reader. In the congressional hearing summaries I used to edit, *UN* and *USAF* ("United Nations" and "U.S. Air Force") were not spelled out. They didn't need to be explained to the reader. The wider the audience, however, the more important it is to make sure that any abbreviations used will be intelligible. If the abbreviations don't aid communication, they don't belong. *The Associated Press Stylebook* is a good guide to the use of unexplained abbreviations. It states, for example, that *UN* need not be spelled out the first time it is used, but that it should be spelled out somewhere in the story.

Memorize This …

Shorthand terms not known to the reader pose a bigger problem for writers and editors. If a concept represented by a long string of words (such as "Space-Based Infrared System," abbreviated as *SBIRS*) is going to be needed throughout a work, then it should be introduced early and—if the work is long—explained again from time to time, such as at the beginning of each section. Spelling out a term once may not be enough in a book, which probably won't be read in one sitting. A reader who puts a volume aside for hours or days may well forget what your abbreviations stand for, so it's helpful to reintroduce the terms and to include them in a list at the front or back of the book.

At the other extreme, some writers use both the spelled-out and abbreviated forms every time. The reader doesn't need to be told time and again that the initials of the Central Intelligence Agency are *CIA* or that the Occupational Health and Safety Administration is known by the acronym *OSHA*. Also, if a term is used only once, why tell the reader how it's abbreviated? When editing a document, I use only the spelled-out forms for terms used just once or twice, except in those rare instances when including the abbreviation may help the reader—as with "deoxyribonucleic acid," for example. Adding the abbreviation *DNA*—or even just using the initials without spelling out the words—may increase the reader's understanding.

Remember, however, that every time you introduce a new abbreviation, you are asking the reader to memorize something else in order to understand the rest of your document. Is that going to enhance communication? Use the shortened form only if the answer is yes.

In *Writing User-Friendly Documents*, the Plain Language Action Network[184] gave some good advice.

> In general, use abbreviations only to refer to terms that are central to the document. For example, if a document is about the Comprehensive Environmental Response, Compensation, and Liability Act, you can refer to it as CERCLA. But do not abbreviate terms that you use only one or a few times. Write them out each time. And whatever you do, don't overwhelm your reader with strings of acronyms and abbreviations.

Capitalization[185]

Do you ever go home, turn on the Air Conditioning and watch TeleVision? You shouldn't. Those are common nouns and shouldn't be capitalized. Initials (such as AC and TV) don't necessarily stand for proper nouns, though often they do: NY, YMCA, USA. A common fault in technical writing is to capitalize phrases such as *commercial off-the-shelf* and *very high frequency* because their initials are capitalized when the words are abbreviated. Another common mistake is to assume that the same letters must be capitalized as in the abbreviation—*Extensible Markup Language*, for example, is abbreviated XML, but the first word is *Extensible*, not *eXtensible*, as it is sometimes written.

Initials for new words tend to start out as all capitals. The initials may eventually see common use in lower case (such as *mph*) or, if they form an acronym (a pronounceable word), even make it into the dictionary (as in the case of *scuba*). Even some acronyms that look like proper nouns, such as *loran*, have made it into the dictionary as common nouns. *Merriam-Webster's Collegiate Dictionary*, 10th edition, says that the word *loran* has been in use since 1932.

It would be simple but simplistic to assume that the words come first and are later shortened; in many cases words are chosen because they will yield a catchy acronym. Take JOVIAL (Joules' own version of international algorithmic language), for example. It's hard to believe that the words *own version* would be used in the name if they weren't needed to compose the acronym JOVIAL (it could just as well have been called "Joules' international algorithmic language").

Many abbreviations, especially initials, are normally printed in capital letters (or in SMALL CAPITALS). Remember, though, that the capitalization of the words will not necessarily correspond to the letters in an acronym. *MADD* ("Mothers Against Drunk Drivers") is an acronym that precisely matches the words in the name, and because it is a proper name, each word is capitalized when the name is spelled out. *MARC* originally stood for "Maryland Rail Commuter," and the *A* in *MARC* was capitalized even though it didn't stand for a word. Later the name was changed to Maryland Area Regional Commuter. Sometimes the abbreviation is a real stretch, as in the case of *UFO* for "Ultrahigh-Frequency Follow-on Satellite"; obviously the initials were chosen for attention-getting reasons rather than to accurately represent the words they stand for.

What about names with capital letters in the middle of them? In his book *No Uncertain Terms*, William Safire had a chapter called "JammedTogetherNames Inc." in which he asked, "How do we handle this manipulation of our media by marketeers who want to catch our attention with tricky typography?" He preferred "*The New York Times*'s solution. From the *Times*'s stylebook: 'Contrived spelling in which the letters are capitalized should not be used unless the second portion of the name is a proper noun.' ... *BankAmerica* is O.K., but *NationsBank* is written *Nationsbank* because 'America' is a proper name and 'bank' is not."[186] I prefer that, too.

Communication

All this acronym soup has one purpose: communication. Keep that in mind when you choose to use any kind of abbreviation in place of more readily understood words. The form of any writing should encourage it to be read. It shouldn't say, "Everybody knows this," or "Memorize this," unless that helps the reader understand it.

Initially Redundant[187]

The automated teller machine machine and the personal identification number number are two common redundancies spawned by electronic banking. Almost every day you hear (or worse, read) about an ATM machine or a PIN number. (Publishing has its equivalent, the ISBN number, or International Standard Book Number number.)

The multitude of capital letters substituting for words nowadays has created an explosion of redundancies because writers couple the shortened versions to words without thinking about the meaning.

It's dismaying to find even Tom Clancy, the preeminent technical writer of fiction, repeatedly referring to "HARM missiles" in his book *Carrier*. (HARM missiles are High-Speed Anti-Radiation Missile missiles.)

Elsewhere we have the GPS system (the Global Positioning System system), the IC community (the Intelligence Community community), LEA agencies (law enforcement agency agencies), and a whopper of a redundancy, the GLONASS satellite navigation system (the Global Navigation Satellite System satellite navigation system).

It seems that many writers are not only forgetting the literal meanings of ordinary words but also the literal meanings of the abbreviations they bandy about. Instead of giving precise meaning in a small space, they add words without adding meaning—and that's a failure to communicate.

More Steps to Better Writing[188]

Kill All the Clichés

Copy editor Laura Moyer recalled an occasion when she tried to eliminate a cliché.

> A few weeks ago I pointed out to a writer that "to be or not to be" has been used already, and it might not be an effective first sentence in the 21st century. I further pointed out that the same phrase was set to appear on the same page in the same edition of the paper, also in a lead sentence.
>
> The writer's response? To request that the other lead be changed. And that's what happened.
>
> But one "to be or not to be" lead still made it into print. Outcome: unsatisfactory.[189]

Trite, overused expressions often get put onto paper without thought. One I see sometimes is reference to "the media" as if the news and communications media were some organized conspiracy that reports only the opinions of one's opponents. One advertisement for a radio show said it would "feature information that you won't find in the media"—as if a radio show weren't part of the media.

Writing without thinking is bad for communication.

Get Rid of the Empty Words

Delete words that don't say anything (known as pleonasm—"more words than those necessary to denote mere sense," according to Merriam-Webster;[190] "an army of words escorting a corporal of thought," according to Ambrose Bierce[191]). Two examples:

> ... such as engineering, manpower, production, computer time, facilities, and the like

> The company is in the process of helping to build its infrastructure, security awareness and marketing

In the first quotation, the reader doesn't need to be told twice (with the phrases *such as* and *and the like*) that these are examples—a partial list. In the second example, the phrase *in the process of* adds no information. *In the process of, currently, in nature, that are, the year* (as in *the year 2013*), and similar phrases usually can be struck with no loss of meaning while improving readability. "We are currently in the process of creating documents that are readable in nature for publication in the year 2015" becomes "We are creating readable documents for publication in 2015."

Without the clutter of empty words, the examples above would become shorter and more readable.

> ... such as engineering, manpower, production, computer time, and facilities

> The company is helping to build its infrastructure, security awareness, and marketing.

However, "the one-sentence advisers you encounter in books and on Twitter—'Omit needless words!' 'When you meet an adverb, kill it!'—will not be of much help to you," wrote *Baltimore Sun* copy editor John McIntyre. "You will of course find it necessary to lance and drain the copy, but indiscriminate bloodletting is not good for the patient."[192]
The Yahoo! Style Guide recommends cutting length, not clarity.

> Some small words that seem unnecessary to native English speakers may be cues that aid comprehension for people less fluent in English. If your audience is likely to include nonnative speakers ... retain *cues that add clarity* ...
>
> Keep the word *that*, especially when it introduces a clause.[193]

Be Specific
Replace vague words with words that give information.

> CIAC's recent report on Russia's aeronautical test facilities

More specifically,

> CIAC's 1994 report on Russia's aeronautical test facilities

What about this phrase?

> by expanding the essential contributions we make to a variety of programs

How does an editor fix that? You can't tell what the essential contributions are or what the variety of programs includes. A phrase like that warrants a note to the author requesting more information.

Read Your Writing and Editing

Examine what you've written or edited. Sometimes things get garbled and come out meaning the opposite of what was intended. Make sure you've ended up with what you meant to say and that the edited words are really better than what you started with.

> No launches were conducted from the proposed Svobodny Cosmodrome.

Not surprising. Launches from a "proposed" cosmodrome would be hard to accomplish.

Sentences in Circles

Avoid needless repetition. Some phrases or sentences are like carousels. They make you dizzy as they go round and round, passing (or making) the same point over and over. A few circular phrases:

> checks on data to verify data accuracy

> a conference complex for conferences

> operational support in support of operations

Is It Silly Season Yet?

Some things just sound funny. Watch your writing for unintentional puns or absurd word pictures.

> signed a 5-year lease ... (with annual escalators and cancellation options) to relocate our ... offices from the 2nd to the 1st floor [It sounds like the escalators help people move from one floor to another.]

> Collective protection equipment (CPE) "is any structure that provides CW-safe areas for personnel rest and recuperation, latrines, showers, and dining." Some CPE is designed to permit all functions simultaneously [You can shower, dine, and use the latrine simultaneously? Yuck!]

> laboratories that had the potential for explosive growth [The labs go boom!]

Two books full of funny examples ("flubs from the nation's press") are *Red Tape Holds Up New Bridge* by Gloria Cooper and *Squad Helps Dog Bite Victim*, featuring excerpts from the *Columbia Journalism Review*.[194]

8

Editorial Relationships

No, I'm not talking about editors in love. I thought it would be worthwhile to discuss how editors professionally relate to other people in publishing. I won't dare to say I have any wisdom to offer, but I could show off a few lumps acquired in the school of editorial hard knocks.

At a few writers conferences at which I served on the faculty, the editors were assembled for a panel discussion. One question often posed by the conferees was "What do you wish you had known when you were starting out?"

The best answer I came up with, and one I used ever afterwards: I wish I had known how little I knew. A little education and a little experience and a little success as a writer fooled me into thinking I knew a lot. No doubt I was happy to be fooled.

Fortunately it wasn't hard to encounter people who knew a lot more than I did, and they were usually patient, generous, and encouraging as they shared what they knew and helped turn me into a professional. As Brendan Gill said, "So I did learn; I go on learning" (see chapter four).

One thing I learned was to take advantage of opportunities to acquire knowledge and experience. For years I had only temporary editing assignments, and they gave me chances to use different style guides, different publishing software, and different quality-control procedures. Regular jobs gave me more chances to work with artists, typesetters, writers, and other editors, and all of them knew things I didn't.

After thirty-plus years of writing and editing, at least I've learned that there is still a lot I don't know. And I've learned that sometimes I'm wrong. That's a helpful attitude to have when working with others.

I've also learned that there are accepted standards of design, writing, editing, and publishing that have been proven to work, that are considered best practices. These things can change, but I continue to advocate them as standards. Sometimes we get to follow best practices, and sometimes we don't. Once, when I was taking a design class for editors, the question arose of the obstacles we face at work. I mentioned "enforced low quality" and got knowing nods and groans from some of the other students. Sometimes we're told what to capitalize, what words to use, even not to question something that was written (which doesn't leave much room for editing). Such times are disappointing and frustrating, and I inject as much quality as I can get away with.

Other things are simply wrong—plagiarism, false advertising—and when we encounter these we have to dig in our heels and say no.

So our professional relationships in publishing ought to be guided, I think, by three principles.

1. We don't know everything, and sometimes we're wrong.
2. We do know, or can learn, best practices in publishing and then follow and advocate them.
3. We should reject false communication such as plagiarism and intentional misinformation.

As professionals, we should be patient, generous, and encouraging, just as others have been to us.

The section "Workers on Copy and Proof" in *Words Into Type* and most of Arthur Plotnik's book *The Elements of Editing* provide useful details of the roles in the publishing process and how they interact.

Working With Authors

Working with an author can be rewarding. It can also be vexing. It was certainly more difficult when I thought I knew more than I did. We need to remember that we editors were put on this earth to help writers.

Aside from their presumed writing ability, authors are as varied as the rest of humanity. Some are meticulous and follow instructions precisely. One writer I worked with routinely turned in copy that was not only well written but was 750 words exactly. When his text was pasted into the layout, usually it would flow into the copy area and end exactly at the bottom of the last column. Other authors have written things tolerably well but paid little or no attention to the publisher's specifications and instructions. Most writers I've worked with have been somewhere in between.

"When the author is an experienced writer and the manuscript gives evidence of having been meticulously prepared, the copy editor will usually not quibble ..." states *Words Into Type*.[195] Indeed editors are happy to see meticulously prepared manuscripts, and authors who have done a thorough job are usually happy to have their work carefully edited. Many writers who trusted my work have given me a free hand to edit what they have produced.

Generally I give new writers the benefit of the doubt—that is, I handle their writing as gently as I do the work of experienced writers. Often a new writer displays abundant talent and needs only some coaching and superficial corrections. Other writers need a lot of help, and it's best to give it with patience and encouragement, though I certainly have fallen short at times. Also, some writers are, well, touchy. They may be insecure about their writing, and they may take correction as a kind of rejection. Even ordinary queries may be received with hostility or interpreted in a way you would not have guessed. One time I spelled out a set of initials in a manuscript but wasn't positive that I had gotten it right, so in my queries to the author I asked something like, "Is this what LG stood for?" The author was an authority on his subject and thought I was questioning his interpretation of LG rather than simply asking whether I had gotten the name correct. ("I wish the creatures wouldn't be so easily offended!" said Alice while in Wonderland.)

One way to help writers understand our queries is to suggest alternatives. If a sentence is unintentionally ambiguous, we can spell out its possible meanings, suggest an unambiguous alternative, and ask whether that would be correct.

We can't always guess how our comments might be provoking, but editors should not be easily offended. True, I am sometimes a stubborn, cranky curmudgeon of an editor, and I suspect there might be a few others like me. I aim to be patient, generous, and encouraging, but I don't always hit the target.

Liz Broomfield, in her LibroEditing blog, proposed four resolutions for editors. I have room for improvement in all four areas.

1. Try to build trust first of all—I already send links to my references, and many of my clients come via recommendation—and I have a new procedure whereby I send the style sheet I've put together during the editing process to the author at the end, thus proving I know what I'm doing and there are reasons for my choices.

2. Remain kind. Sometimes I do get a little exasperated. But I, too, make the same mistakes throughout, repeat myself and am not always consistent. So why should I expect anyone else to be any different?

3. Understand that when the client asks a question, sometimes they just need reassurance that they're not stupid or rubbish at writing. And they are almost never casting doubt on my ability, but either wanting to know why in order to make their writing better, or being anxious generally.

4. Make sure I praise as well as criticise. I do try to do this already; I will try to do it more, now. Whether they've written a great bibliography or coined a smart turn of phrase, even if they've just managed to avoid plagiarising or quoting Wikipedia this time round, there's always something to praise and I must find it and mention it.[196]

Working With Publishers

Publishers are usually the bosses of editors. They run the gamut of ability, experience, and personality, just as authors do. Some are publications people who have come up through the ranks or have otherwise acquired solid knowledge of editing, design, marketing, and people, and they have a good dollop of business sense as well. Others have little idea of editing, design, marketing, or how to manage people, and sometimes have little business sense either. As with authors, most publishers are somewhere in between.

A good publisher will give you room to be a professional while necessarily imposing restrictions to accommodate competing concerns, such as design, marketing, personnel management, and finance. Even if you have a good publisher, remember that this person is only a human being who, like you, will make mistakes, really mess things up sometimes, and possibly offend somebody. Even if your boss is an amateur publisher who decides things according to personal preference or even a whim, this person still can probably see things you can't and may even respond to helpful suggestions from you. A bad publisher will make poor decisions and make sure that you get blamed when things fall apart.

If you aren't the boss, remember that, no matter which kind of boss you have, you still have to accommodate what the publisher wants, and you may have to live with the situation if you can't find something better.

Also, while we want to do the best job we can in our professional environment, there may well be limits (if only in the range of content we work on—it might be technical manuals, for example) that don't allow us to use all our talents and skills. If that's the case, I recommend finding additional areas working with the English language to express yourself, such as freelance writing or volunteer editing for a charity's publication.

Evan Morris "worked for a major New York City law firm … as a legal assistant and proofreading supervisor" and "probably read several thousand merger agreements, tender offers, [Securities and Exchange Commission] registration statements, and briefs. Most of this literature was deadly dull."[197] He went on to better things, though: He now writes the syndicated Word Detective column, carrying on where his parents left off, and has written several books.

As a patient, generous, encouraging editor, you might also find opportunities to help others display their talents. When I worked at ANSER, I found myself for at least the second time in my career working with a lot of graphic designers. I thought that they might have produced some art outside of work and would like to display it for their co-workers. I helped organize a company art show, and it turned out that lots of employees besides the staff artists had items to enter. It gave people a chance to exhibit creative work that the other employees don't usually see, and it helped us all to appreciate one another's talents.

Working With Artists

You might have heard that artists are fussy, temperamental eccentrics. However, in my own experience, I have learned lessons in patience, generosity, and encouragement from the artists I've worked with. (Maybe I'm just such a grouch that they shine by comparison.) I don't think I've ever asked one of them for help and not gotten it in abundance; one sat patiently with me and gave me lessons in PageMaker and Quark Xpress.

Some artists are so focused on design that they won't notice big, honking typos (which is where we editors come in); some are good at art *and* English and will notice areas where the writing can be improved (as did Elaine Sapp, who balked at the wordy "No Parking" signs).

With the fast design work that is sometimes possible thanks to computers, many clients also focus so much on the design that they neglect the writing, wanting to see how something is going to look before the text is edited (if it ever gets edited). A sequence of work from the pre-computer days of publishing still is valuable: writing first, editing second, layout third. If a document is designed and laid out before the text is edited, it complicates the editing task, because now the writing must be edited not only for things such as focus, content, grammar, and precise language, but for length as well, sometimes within very strict limits.

Working With Readers

Working with readers? The recipients, consumers, and beneficiaries of our editing? Yes. While we don't work with readers directly the way we work with authors, publishers, or artists, we may become involved with them. Readers sometimes send the publisher criticism, corrections, or questions, all of which must be answered politely, and in fact the publisher probably wants to keep those communications coming, because they provide marketing information about publications and help us avoid repeating errors.

Some newspapers, such as *The New York Times* and *The Washington Post*, occasionally host online chats during which readers can ask questions of the editors. Both readers and editors seem to benefit from and enjoy these exchanges.

Managing Expectations

"Steve-O, Steve-O!" one of my co-workers likes to say. She doesn't want my attention. "It just feels good to say that."

Other people have come into the office asking for galley proofs or a technical edit but had no idea what those things were. Maybe it just feels good to say "galley proofs" and "tech edit." Those words do sound important. As Richard Mitchell, the Underground Grammarian, pointed out, "We like to think, or at least we like others to think, that what we do is important and difficult and that we achieve it only out of skill and intelligence. ... we seize gratefully any opportunity to *sound* as though we were skillful and intelligent."[198]

One writer wanted "light editing." To find out what the person wanted done, I called him and started reading items from our copyediting checklist (see chapter nine, "The Editor's Tools"): "Read every job twice," "Check the date," "Check the letterhead ..." "Check the page numbers," "Check the copyright statement," "Check chapter titles or article titles (and page numbers) against the table of contents ..." His responses were, No, no, no, yes (to checking the page numbers), no, no ... and "Don't change anything I wrote." (So he actually wanted no editing done.) Unfortunately the document was strewn with misspellings, wrong names, and misused words. And the date on the cover was wrong.

Another person wanted a "tech edit only." Since a technical edit is just about the most thorough editing possible (see "Editorial Tasks" in chapter nine), I asked what this person *didn't* want done. That produced a huffy response and a promise not to bother me again. I explained that it wasn't a bother; I just wanted to know what work was desired.

To find out what people really want, I need to see whether we are using common terms. Sometimes people ask me for a review of a document. I refer them to a list of editing tasks. Do they want comments only? Some do. Do they want suggested edits, marked on paper, which they will choose whether to use? Some do. Sometimes they say they want a review when they want editing. Sometimes they say they want editing when they want only a superficial check before printing. It helps for the editor to get these things clarified so that both writer and editor know what is expected.

■■ 9 ■■

The Editor's Tools

Editing for content, focus, precise language, and grammar—in short, policing what goes into print—is a job that requires professionalism and resources. Like other police, we sometimes have to call for backup.

The well-equipped editor depends on tools, procedures, and resources.

Tools

Style Sheets

Most style choices (see the discussion of "house style" in chapter five) are governed by the style guide used by the publisher. Beyond that, however, most manuscripts—especially book-length ones—involve more choices: for example, whether to capitalize *Arctic*, or whether to include metric equivalents of English measurements.

The editor records such decisions in alphabetical order on a style sheet, which then stays with the manuscript throughout production so that typesetters and proofreaders will have ready answers for questions of inconsistency that arise.

It is best to begin the style sheet *after* reading through the manuscript. Settling a minor inconsistency based on the first few pages may create more work than necessary: a variation, such as *Arctic* capitalized, may appear to predominate at first but appear less frequently throughout the remainder of the text.

Checklists

Another important editor's tool is the checklist. There are simply too many aspects to consider in any editing job for most individuals to keep track of mentally. For example, in periodicals, the issue date, copyright date, and other information that is printed in every issue could be wrong. When some pages are reused from issue to issue, there's always a danger of pages going to press with an old date on them. Therefore a checklist for editing and proofreading is invaluable. It is entirely possible to read a passage several times and not notice that there are double quotation marks within double quotation marks, or two opening parentheses but only one closing, or a proper name spelled two different ways. I personally have no trouble missing these things. After editing a piece of writing, the best thing to do is to look through it item by item for errors, discrepancies, and inconsistencies. A sample editing checklist follows, with annotation; most editors will want to customize their own.

A Sample Copy-Editing and Proofreading Checklist

____ Read the proof word for word against the original copy (if provided). (Most jobs don't have a correct original, but this applies to quotations, too.)

____ Read the proof straight through without checking against the original. (In any event, read every job twice.)

____ Check the date.

____ Check the letterhead or other headings that contain standard information.

____ Check the page numbers.

____ Check the copyright statement. (Refer to the contract or other legal documents, if appropriate.)

____ Check chapter titles or article titles (and page numbers) against the table of contents.

____ Check chapter and section numbering.

____ Check figure and table numbering.

____ Check subheads for consistency (e.g., all caps, upper and lower cases, or initial caps). Also check their format (e.g., indention and font) and numbering.

___ Check running heads (headings repeated at the tops of pages).

___ Check proper names to be sure they are consistently spelled and capitalized.

___ Check superscripts against footnotes or endnotes to be sure they correspond and to be sure none are missing.

___ Check jumps and cross-references. (A jump is a continuation of text somewhere else; a cross-reference indicates material elsewhere in the document, such as "See figure 3.")

___ Check captions.

___ Check quotation marks to be sure that all are paired and that there are no doubles within doubles.

___ Check parentheses to be sure that all are paired and that there are no parentheses within parentheses.

___ Check arithmetic, such as columns of numbers and pie charts.

___ Check quotations word for word against source material to be sure they correspond precisely.

___ Check for widows and orphans. (A widow is a word or fragment of a word on a line by itself at the end of a paragraph or the end of a page; an orphan is a word or fragment of a word on a line by itself at the top of a page. Microsoft Word has built-in widow and orphan control, but graphics and tables can interfere with it.)

___ Check for more than two consecutive lines ending with hyphens. (Some word-processing and layout programs automatically limit this.)

___ Check series of words or phrases for parallel construction. (For example, in a bulleted list, every item might be the completion of a sentence at the end of the paragraph above, or maybe they should all be complete sentences on their own.)

___ Check paragraph indents for consistency.

___ Watch for font and size changes.

___ Run a spell-check on the file, if possible.

___ In justified copy, watch for excessively tight or loose lines. ("Justified" means aligned to the margins. "Left justified" or "right justified," also called "flush left" and "flush right," mean aligned to only one margin or the other.)

___ Place a check mark next to any verified proper names (when editing on paper).

_____ Check bleeds, trim, and gutters. (This applies to preparing documents for printing. A bleed involves printing on oversize paper and then trimming it; in that case it must be printed beyond the margin where it will be trimmed. The trim is the edge where the paper will be cut; items too close to the edge can get lopped off, and this applies as well to how close to the edge of the paper things can be printed. The gutter is the white space in the center of two pages; thick books with perfect binding—that is, glued to a spine—need more gutter.)

_____ Check for end-of-story dingbats (typographical ornaments—if the document uses them).

_____ Make sure paragraphs have ending punctuation.

_____ Make sure bulleted or numbered lists comprise at least two items. (A numbered list should go beyond 1.)

_____ Search for bad words (my slang term for correctly spelled words that usually do not belong but often go unnoticed, e.g., *asses, polices, mange, pubic, posses,* and *statue*).

_____ Search for hidden text. (Text in Word can be hidden; it shows up when paragraph marks and other nonprinting items are shown, and it can be found using Word's Find function.)

_____ Check classification markings (if a document is classified or otherwise restricted).

_____ Check hyperlinks.

_____ Check the head commands in HTML files.

_____ Check repeated information (for example, facts that appear in more than one place: Do they say the same thing?).

Spell-Checkers

A spell-checker is an invaluable tool for on-screen editing. It is a very good idea to run a final spell-check after the editing is finished; it helps locate mistakes introduced during editing. The spell-checker in Microsoft Word gives the editor the choice of ignoring words that contain numbers. I do not tell the spell-checker to ignore anything. A word, such as *Y2K* (if you can call that a word), containing a number is not automatically correct—check out these requirements for an administrative assistant, posted in a want ad: "Must be capable of 	typing technical narrative and data."

■■ Hazards of Word's AutoCorrect

AutoCorrect in Microsoft Word is set to automatically change *(c)* to ©, which can turn a 501(c)(3) nonprofit corporation into a 501©(3). Check any settings in your software that may automatically replace things that aren't wrong.

Another hazardous AutoCorrect feature in Word is "Correct TWo INitial CApitals." If left on, this will alter abbreviations such as *BEd* (bachelor of education) into *Bed*. "Capitalize first letter of sentences" will turn *Dunham et al. have not approved this* into *Dunham et al. Have not approved this*, mistaking the period in *et al.* for the end of a sentence.

"Replace as you type … Ordinals (1st) with superscript" is another AutoCorrect default. It changes *21st century* into *21st century*. Not since the mid-1800s have superscripts been in vogue with ordinal numbers, so why Microsoft Word has this style for a default is a mystery. *Words Into Type* points out that "superscripts are used for exponents (2^3), for the mass number of isotopes (^{235}U), and for footnote or bibliographic references (Smith [9, 10])."[199] It doesn't mention ordinal numbers; superscript ordinals are passé.

■■ Other Uses of the Spell-Checker[200]

Besides pausing at every misspelled word, the spell-checker pauses at every unknown proper name and abbreviation. You can use this to your advantage. When it stops at a proper name, if you're sure it's spelled correctly, click on "Ignore All." Then watch for different versions of the same name. This procedure has saved me countless times, spotting, for example, (Senator) Arlen "Spector" after I'd verified that "Specter" was correct.

The spell-checker can also find abbreviations used only once or twice. The first time it comes to an unknown term, such as MDR ("medium data rate"), I click "Ignore" and make a note of it. If it appears three times or more, I click "Ignore All." Otherwise I spell it out in the one or two places the spell-checker found it. This technique won't work if you add those abbreviations to your computer's personal dictionary.

Editing on Paper or On-Screen?[201]

Both methods have their advantages. Generally I prefer to edit on-screen, but I find it easier to spot errors on paper, so even when I edit on-screen I like to print out a final copy to read. Conversely, even when all editorial changes must be recorded on paper, I like to get a copy of the file so that I can search for repeated terms and cross-references, and so that I can run a spell-check.

Here's an example of how having a copy of the computer file saves time and energy (even when you're editing on paper): Work in the computer file to reduce the quantity of abbreviations in the text, because a reader must know or memorize them in order to comprehend the writing. One choice is to spell out abbreviations the first time they're used and to eliminate abbreviations not used more than twice. It's much easier to find the first appearance of a term by searching with the Find function in a word-processing program than to page through a long document looking for words. Terms inconsistently spelled are easier to find electronically, too. When I see *roadmap* and ask myself, "Didn't I see it as *road map* earlier in the document?" it's easy to search for the word both ways and to make it consistent. "Global" changes—such as making straight apostrophes into typographical ones—can be accomplished in a few seconds. Extra spaces can be deleted in one swoop, whereas two spaces at the end of a line in flush-left text can't even be seen on a printout. When a sentence needs to be rearranged, electronic cutting and pasting takes a small fraction of the time required to mark transpositions on paper. On the whole, on-screen editing is faster.

Paper copies are usually more legible, however, and are better for comparing pages side by side. If subheads are formatted inconsistently, I can spot this problem more easily on paper. Sometimes it's easier to mark queries on paper, too, rather than to highlight them in the document file.

Editing on paper, however, requires room to write. If only paper copies are available for editing, ask that the document be double-spaced. The editor's and author's jobs become harder when we have to cram notations between single-spaced lines.

Editing on paper is not the only way to have a paper record of editing changes. When editing on-screen, I normally save a new version of the file to work on. That not only provides a backup of the original, but also permits the author or editor to use Word's Compare Documents or Track Changes features to automatically highlight changes.

Procedures

These are techniques that, in my experience, have worked pretty well. Most important, I think, is to create a system and use it. I've often been told, "Do your magic." I sometimes answer, "The only magic I know is how to make things disappear." Editing works best as a system, not a magic show. Read everything twice; create and use a checklist; and, as EEI (formerly Editorial Experts, Inc.) taught me, don't ditch the system when things get tight.

Editorial Tasks[202]

"Writing should be so clear to the reader the first time it's read," said editor Margaret Palm, "that the reader should never have to go back and read something twice to understand it."

If something can be read two ways, somebody somewhere will read it the wrong way. A "cooler is not a large system impact ..." stated one document I edited. I queried the author: "Does this mean 'a cooler would not have a large impact on the system' or 'a cooler does not have an impact on large systems'?" The reader might have read it only one way or not understood it at all.

The editor looks for things that are perfectly clear to the writer but not clear to others, and makes sure that the writer will be understood.

Copy editor Laura Moyer gave an example on her Red Pen blog:

> A reader wrote to critique a line from our editorial on Congress' last-minute agreement to avoid defaulting on our national debt.
> She said she had to read this sentence three times before she got it:
> "Republicans elected last year to correct the accumulation of a mountain of federal debt refused to vote for a debt-ceiling increase without some heavy strings attached."[203]

After examining suggested solutions that involved commas, Moyer concluded:

> Something like this might have worked better:
> "Republicans elected ~~(or re-elected)~~ last year to correct ~~what many voters saw as a precipitous slide to the left and~~ the accumulation of a mountain of federal debt refused to vote for a debt-ceiling increase without some heavy strings attached."[204]

Editor Dave Fessenden would have gone further, and I agree: "My problem with this example is that Moyer failed to remove the most ambiguous part of the sentence: the word *elected*. I'm still not entirely sure that these Republicans were elected (as in voted into office) or if they elected (as in made a choice). Did voters elect these Republicans in the hope that they would correct the accumulating debt, or did these Republicans choose to correct the accumulating debt? I'm assuming it's the former, so here's how I would have rewritten it:

> Republicans (who were elected last year on the promise that they would correct the accumulation of a mountain of federal debt) refused …

"Actually, I probably would have rewritten it even more than that."

> Republicans (true to their campaign promise to deal with accumulating federal debt) refused …

Besides such editing for clarity, editors may be called on for many pre-publication tasks: creating bibliographies or indexes,* for example, or choosing pull quotes and writing headlines. The bulk of the editor's work, however, can be summarized in five editorial tasks: *substantive editing, copy editing, technical editing, proofreading,* and *quality checks.*

Substantive editing examines content and organization as well as the writing itself. Should chapter five be the first chapter instead? Should some technical material be moved to an appendix? Is any material lacking or treated in too much detail? It may involve removing redundant wording, clarifying confusing text, and rewriting. Because substantive editing often involves revisions, it takes more time, both for the editor and the author. If this level of editing is required, be sure to allow time for additional work on the document.

Although large publishing houses have both editors and copy editors, in most smaller publishing organizations substantive editing includes copy editing.

Copy editing covers the details of writing: punctuation, grammar, capitalization, word choice, redundancy, repetitiveness, accuracy, and consistency. Spelling and capitalizing words consistently (*totalled* vs. *totaled,* or *Federal* vs. *federal*) makes reading easier and helps communication. Copy-editing style generally involves choosing among two or more acceptable ways of spelling or capitalizing words. The Government Printing Office style, for example, says to use numerals

---

* "A good index is a form of *writing;* it requires the application of a human mind, which can see meanings where a computer sees only words," wrote Jack Lyon in "The Little Man Who Wasn't There" on the blog An American Editor, March 13, 2013.

with all units of measure but spell out numbers up to ten in all other uses (so GPO style calls for "four computers" but "5 hours").

In copy editing, editors should also check arithmetic, verify bibliographical information when possible, make sure that headings are numbered correctly, and check cross-references (for instance, if you come across "See Figure 3," check to make sure there is a Figure 3 and whether it shows what the text says it shows). In addition, copy editors keep an eye on details such as area codes, zip codes, place names, and dates.

Copy editing frequently turns up questions that only the author can answer: A column of numbers doesn't add up; is the total wrong or is one of the other elements incorrect? A source's name is spelled two different ways; which one is correct? A set of initials isn't spelled out anywhere; what does it stand for? Copy-edited work is often returned to the author with some questions, so allow time for the author to find the answers and make any necessary changes.

Technical editing involves making sure the work "is technically accurate—no errors in the text or in any non-text elements (for example, illustrations and tables)," wrote Jean Hollis Weber on her Technical Editors' Eyrie website.[205] According to Weber, a technical editor will:

1. "Check and verify all facts and references. ..."
2. "Ensure consistency. ..."
3. "Check and verify all graphics, figures, listings, tables and other non-text items. ..."
4. "Process and track all screen shots. ..."
5. "Answer all queries of a technical nature. ..."
6. "Ensure the work meets market and audience goals. ..."

Another editorial task is *proofreading*, which means comparing typeset copy against a correct original. If you rarely receive completely correct originals, you won't do much proofreading. Examples of material that all editors need to proofread are quotations, which must be reproduced precisely, and equations or formulae, which likewise must be copied correctly and sometimes lose important formatting (such as subscripts or Greek characters) in conversion from one program to another. Proofreading is also done to compare typeset copy against the previous version, typically the final manuscript after editing.

Quality checks are done after layout is complete. At this point, the type has been adjusted to fit the layout, the graphics are in place, and the work is almost ready for reproduction. This is not the time to edit, so a quality check normally does not even involve reading the whole document. It involves checking for things that often go wrong in typesetting and layout. Is the table of contents correct? Is the date correct? Are any words broken incorrectly? Do the captions match the illustrations? Are there any unanswered questions? Are all the graphics legible?

How Long Does Editing Take?[206]

EEI Communications gives 750 words per hour as a rule of thumb for copy editing. That's about three double-spaced pages per hour. It includes all the tasks in copy editing, such as reading the document twice, referring to a checklist, and marking queries. When editing on screen, I also normally apply styles so that the text can be made uniform (and the format easily changed) and so that tables of contents can be generated automatically.

Substantive editing takes about twice as long as copy editing; a quality check takes less time, but, again, a quality check does not normally involve reading the document.

Extra tasks, such as verifying quotations, making a bibliography consistent, or editing graphics for legibility, take longer. When I had to look up some cited "criticism" coming from the Government Accountability Office, the criticism turned out to be a four-minute video statement at a Senate hearing. The "quote" in the report I was editing more or less captured the meaning, but the words were in a different order. I must have spent ten or fifteen minutes on that one quote.

Cheap, Quick Quality[207]

Can we produce quality documents quickly and cheaply? A proverb of publishing is that you cannot produce something fast, cheaply, and well. You must choose two out of the three. One analyst who wanted me to skip the spell-check on a rush job said, "Timeliness is more important than accuracy." I disagreed with his statement, but he was tacitly acknowledging that more speed meant lower quality.

However, many managers today say that speed, quality, and economy are compatible. A U.S. Government mantra has been "faster, better, cheaper." Acquisition reform means that the Defense Department meets requirements "by buying smarter and faster and getting better products at a cheaper price," Secretary of Defense William S. Cohen wrote in his 1998 "Annual Report to the President and the Congress."

One example of attempting to do things faster, better, and cheaper with high public visibility involved the National Aeronautics and Space Administration. "Using a management philosophy dubbed 'Faster-Better-Cheaper,' or 'FBC,' NASA tried to develop high-quality, low-cost space missions on short schedules," wrote James Oberg of United Press International in March 2000. "But many projects began failing at an alarming rate," and a specially appointed panel "told NASA the FBC approach wasn't working and needed major changes."

However, space historian Howard McCurdy, professor of public affairs at American University, told Space.com that "faster, better, cheaper" is "a good concept. It's just very difficult to implement and practice. ... In general, it's a cultural problem." (One culture that adopted it was the communist government of East Germany, which in 1955 promulgated the slogan "Better, cheaper, faster."[208])

"'Pick any two,'" McCurdy said, "is the dominant culture in the aerospace industry" but "it's not a fact of life." It is possible, he said, to have speed, quality, and economy. He pointed to "the culture that dominates the new information-age industries ... which is, you can simultaneously improve cost, schedule and performance.... It's why Microsoft was so much better, 20 years ago, than IBM."

"Faster, better, cheaper" is possible, said McCurdy, "if you use the right management techniques and you do the correct engineering, and you do the testing that is necessary—and you don't under-fund the project! In concept, it is a workable system."

McCurdy's comment about not underfunding projects indicates that "faster, better, cheaper" is not necessarily impossible but that there are limits: At some point, reductions in cost and time *will* impinge on quality. Not every project offers opportunities for cost-cutting or schedule reduction. The correct question to be asked, therefore, is "Where do we have room for improvement?"

In publishing, if you don't allow time to spell-check a document, you clearly are sacrificing quality for speed. The point of diminishing returns comes long before that, however. As *Words Into Type*[209] states, "The editor must be alert at all times to inaccuracies and conflicting statements. Geographical features must be carefully checked, an exacting task in some books. Classical, historical, and literary references may be inexact and must be scrutinized. Dates and all references or statements in which there is a time element must be examined with care." And these are only a fraction of the editor's duties listed in *Words Into Type*.

The idea of carefully checking accuracy applies to writing as well as editing. "There are no safe shortcuts," wrote David S. Broder, a political reporter for *The Washington Post*. "... the only way to cover a story is to cover it: to spend as much time with the people as humanly possible, to ask as many questions as they will tolerate, and never to assume I know what is going on without asking."[210]

Undoubtedly there are publications projects that can be done faster, better, *and* cheaper—some projects have room for improvement in all three areas. Achieving quality in publications, however, means following a system, even when time is short. "Things will get out of control," General Lee says in the film *Gettysburg*. "That is why we have orders." Speed, cost, and quality need to be managed—not simply one exchanged for another in a moment of panic. We owe it to our clients not to rush things if it would unacceptably reduce quality.

We also owe it to our clients to look for ways to do our jobs better—faster and cheaper, too. Can we always improve all three? No. Should we try? Yes.

Read for Sense

There are two crucial times to read every piece of writing to see whether it makes sense: on first perusal, so that the author can be queried about inexplicable portions, and during editing, to see whether the editing changes make sense out of the writing.

An editor or proofreader working on the book *Cops and God* (by Detective Steven Rogers with Lloyd Hildebrand) must have had a reflex response to two adjectives in a row, because *white-frame house* was hyphenated in several places. A moment or two of reflection should have produced the realization that a frame house is a type of building and that its exterior, not its frame, might be white. (Overzealousness in hyphenation may have led to laxity in spelling, because *cemetery* was consistently spelled *cematary*.)

I learned the hard way to read through every piece of writing after the editing is complete. I usually find a few places where I have marked a change in the wrong spot, failed to resolve an ambiguity, or made an editing change that produced no good result.

Read Everything Twice

Read everything at least twice—no exceptions. I have noticed literally thousands of errors only on the second (or third) time through a manuscript or proof. This does not include all the errors I missed entirely. If you're editing on paper (rather than on a computer), then the more red ink you put down, the harder it will be to spot the remaining glaring errors.

Compare Repeated Quotations

It is not at all unusual to find that an author has quoted the same material twice but differently. "A successful battle may give us America," Lord Cornwallis is quoted as saying in *The First Salute* by Barbara Tuchman. Those words are the chapter's title, and they appear at the top of every right-hand page in that chapter. Yet on page 209, we read, "The British were no nearer a secure hold on the South or the 'battle [that] will give us America,' though Cornwallis was still bent on achieving it …"—*will* give or *may* give?

Write Neatly

I learned this rule while working at a typesetting company many years ago, just before the desktop publishing revolution allowed people to set their own type. I worked on the night shift, and most of the jobs were due the next morning, and we would sometimes receive work with handwritten instructions that were hard to understand. We did not want to call clients in the middle of the night to ask for more information, so we were grateful when people took the time to print neatly.

That was a long time ago, but often I still receive proofs with written instructions, and sometimes they are hard to read. Sometimes I have to get more information from whoever wrote them, and sometimes the person is not available. I can't do much about that, but I can make sure that my own marks on proof copies are clear. It means writing (better yet, printing) slowly and carefully, but the time spent is repaid by the delays that don't happen and by mistakes that don't get published. Copy editor Laura Moyer recalled an instance when a "page proof with" a "hideous headline error [*Chile* misspelled] had passed under" her "gaze and gone to its destiny." She "marked it and gave it to the paginator." But "my handwriting was lousy," she wrote. "What I wrote looked like 'Chilie.' And that's how the word was corrected."[211]

Office Tips

If you can't get hold of someone by phone or e-mail, you can drop a note in that day's mail. Sometimes phone tag—or e-mail tag—can go on for days. If you make contact before the note arrives in the mail, there's no harm done.

Check files as soon as you receive them. Many times I've had to request replacement files because a disk was bad, the file was corrupted, the file was in a format my software couldn't read, or the file was locked by a password (or so the software said). If you check the file as soon as you receive it, even if you don't plan to work on it for days or weeks, you can discover any damaged files and get replacements before you need to work on them.

Resources

Books

The Associated Press Stylebook and Libel Manual.[212] No matter which style guide your publications follow, the AP style guide is a useful resource. The main part of the book comprises hundreds of pages of alphabetically arranged entries that go far beyond listing AP's preferred spellings (such as *dialogue*, not *dialog*) and abbreviations (*Colo.*, not *CO*, for Colorado) and how to capitalize titles ("capitalize the principal words, including prepositions and conjunctions of four or more letters"). Many entries include explanations of the terms to aid writers and editors in using them correctly. A knot, for example, is defined as one nautical mile per hour and is followed by the multiplier (1.15) to convert knots to miles per hour. *Lawyer* is identified as "a generic term for all members of the bar" and is followed by explanations of the terms *attorney*, *barrister*, *counselor*, *solicitor*, and *solicitor general*. The entry for *Mach number* shows that the *M* is capitalized, gives its derivation (from Ernst Mach), defines *Mach 1* as the speed of sound, and provides a rule of thumb (Mach 1 is about 750 miles per hour at sea level).

The AP guide also directs writers to preserve useful distinctions, such as the narrow meaning of *firm*: "A business partnership is correctly referred to as a *firm*. ... Do not use *firm* in references to an incorporated business entity. Use *the company* or *the corporation* instead."

The AP guide is full of good editorial advice, too.

- "In general, avoid jargon."
- "Do not use abbreviations or acronyms which the reader would not quickly recognize."
- "Never alter quotations."

- On "obscenities, profanities, vulgarities": "Do not use them in stories unless they are part of direct quotations and there is a compelling reason for them."

The guide also explains the differences among many commonly confused words, such as *affect* and *effect*; *anticipate* and *expect*; and *compose, comprise,* and *constitute.*

The *weapons* and *weather terms* entries are followed by subentries with definitions and explanations of additional terms. Separate sections deal with sports and business terms.

Following the alphabetized listings is a guide to punctuation, which begins, "There is no alternative to correct punctuation. Incorrect punctuation can change the meaning of a sentence, the results of which could be far-reaching." Some of the rules, such as the use of serial commas, differ from those promulgated in the Chicago manual, the Government Printing Office manual, or *The Elements of Style*. Nonetheless the AP guide is unexceptionable in its philosophy of punctuation: "The basic guideline is to use common sense."

Finally, the libel manual provides useful information to any writer or editor who is dealing with controversial material, and it briefly covers the Freedom of Information Act, privacy, and copyrights as well.

Unlike some style guides that consist mainly of rules, the AP guide is principally an aid to clarity—something to which every writer and editor should aspire. It's designed to facilitate mass written communication. Available in many bookstores or from Amazon.com, *The Associated Press Stylebook and Libel Manual* is well worth the price.

***The Dictionary of Clichés* by James Rogers** (New York: Ballantine Books, 1985) is a useful reference book. If you can't weed out the clichés, you can at least make sure the writers get them right.

***The Dictionary of Misinformation* and *More Misinformation*, both by Tom Burnam** (Ballantine Books). Why would you want books of misinformation? Not so you can repeat it, but so you can eradicate it from the documents you edit. Like *The Dictionary of Clichés*, these books are paperbacks, available at modest prices.

***The Elements of Editing: A Modern Guide for Editors and Journalists* by Arthur Plotnik** (New York: Macmillan, 1982). This book has helpful discussions of editors and their roles, their craft, and the publications process. The sections on libraries, photography, and electronic editing are sorely out of date, though.

Words Into Type (Prentice-Hall) is my favorite style guide. It covers much of the same ground, and sets forth generally the same rules, as *The Chicago Manual of Style* published by the University of Chicago Press, but I prefer *Words Into Type* for its index and the examples it gives. My copy is the Third Edition (1974), which I have been using for more than thirty years. Some of the information on typesetting is outdated, but the section is worth studying just the same.

The Yahoo! Style Guide: Writing and Editing for the Web (New York: St. Martin's Press, 2010). If you need a handbook on writing and editing for the Web, this is it.

Internet Resources

An American Editor (americaneditor.wordpress.com). This blog, hosted by Richard Adin, is written especially for freelancers but covers many aspects of usage.

Candi On Content (candioncontent.blogspot.com). This blog by Candi Harrison is for government communicators, but her thoughtful advice is helpful for a wide range of publications, and a lot of it applies specifically to nonprofit organizations.

Concept to Contract (fromconcepttocontract.com) is editor Dave Fessenden's blog that focuses on writing for the Christian book market but with lots of helpful discussion for writers and editors in any field.

The Copyeditors' Knowledge Base (www.kokedit.com/ckb.php) hosted by Katharine O'Moore-Klopf covers seven areas: The Basics, Education and Certification, Business Tools, Editing Tools, Networking, Finding Work, and Profession-Related Reading.

The Homework Spot (www.HomeworkSpot.com) offers guidance for research, including a useful section to help determine the reliability of information provided on a website, along with links to other resources on that topic.

The Library Spot (www.libraryspot.com) has a directory of libraries and an online reading room and reference desk.

LibroEditing (libroediting.com) is a blog by Liz Broomfield, covering editing and proofreading.

OneLook Dictionaries (www.onelook.com) searches many dictionaries (including specialized ones) at once.

The Plain Language Action and Information Network (www.plain language.gov) promotes the use of plain language for all government communications, and it offers, among other resources, the Federal Plain Language Guidelines. Its members believe that using plain language will save federal agencies time and money, and provide better service to the American public.

The Purdue Online Writing Lab (owl.english.purdue.edu/owl) offers writing resources and instructional material, such as a guide to the American Psychological Association style.

The Quote Investigator (quoteinvestigator.com) is the website where Garson O'Toole exhaustively investigates the sources of quotations, which are indexed by author (or purported author).

The Technical Editors' Eyrie (www.jeanweber.com/newsite), hosted by Jean Hollis Weber, is a website for technical editors to share knowledge, experiences, and resources.

The Underground Grammarian (www.sourcetext.com/grammarian) is a website dedicated to preserving the works of Richard Mitchell. I was privileged to have him for an English professor at Glassboro State College in New Jersey in the late 1970s. Three books—*Less Than Words Can Say*, *The Leaning Tower of Babel*, and *The Graves of Academe*—incisively skewer the shallow, ill-thought-out use of English, especially in academia. All the books, along with some shorter pieces and the *Underground Grammarian* newsletters, are freely available as electronic files on the Underground Grammarian website.

Webopedia (www.webopedia.com) explains information technology terms.

The Word Detective (www.word-detective.com) is loaded with entertaining discussions of etymology and meaning.

World Wide Words (www.worldwidewords.org) is a fascinating site hosted by a Briton, Michael Quinion, who offers a free weekly e-mail newsletter.

You Don't Say (www.baltimoresun.com/news/language-blog) is a blog with frequent, informative postings by *Baltimore Sun* copy editor John McIntyre.

10

Samples of Editing

This chapter has real-life editing examples with notes about what I changed and why. The first example is the chapter title. It started out as "Editing Samples." I decided that it could be misread to mean "how to edit samples." I hope it's clear enough now.

The next example is an instance of guest editing by Richard Mitchell, from his book *Less Than Words Can Say*. The rest are my work.

Already in Plain English

Mitchell quoted from the "Draft Regulations to Implement the National Environmental Policy Act," noting that it had already "been rewritten into what they call plain English."

> The agency need make the finding of no significant impact available for public review for thirty days before the agency makes its final determination whether to prepare an environmental impact statement and before the action may begin only in one of the following limited circumstances: …

"In effect," Mitchell said, "it says that the agency need do something only under certain circumstances. That's a clear thought." But "thirty-four words intervene between 'need' and 'only,'" and there's "something that sounds like a modification but isn't: 'impact available for public review.' … the tedious parade of words and clauses not yet related to any idea that we can identify [makes it] awkward, puzzling, and exasperating. …

"The idea is not complicated; the prose, in fact, is not complicated—it's just bad. Nevertheless, it *could* be simplified even using that vocabulary. Here's how it might go:"

> In some cases, a finding of no significant impact does have to be made available for public review. Public review means that you have to give the public thirty days to look it over before you can even decide whether to write an environmental impact statement, and certainly before any action is taken. Here are the cases in which you do have to provide the public review:[213]

Word Use: *Tout*

> Long touted as a successful model for economic growth in Asia, South Korea's economy experienced many years of enviable success. But in the last several years …

I changed *touted* to *pointed to*. *Tout* has two meanings: (1) to praise or (2) to praise with false intent (its original meaning, which persists).[214] Because of the ambiguity, it's better not to use it unless the implication is clear. In this case, the sentence that follows says that South Korea's economy isn't all it's cracked up to be, so the touting may well involve sly deception—or maybe not. This was somewhat of a guess on my part, so I queried it with an explanation. It was published with the words *pointed to* instead of *touted*. Maybe John McIntyre's blog entry on *tout*, which I sent along with the edited file, had something to do with my change being accepted. McIntyre, copy editor at *The Baltimore Sun*, wrote that a tout is "someone who solicits custom, recommends, or even importunes, like the gentleman outside a strip bar extolling the delights within." That should be enough to discourage a serious writer from using the word lightly.

Awkward Wording

> **Original:** historical caparisons of former first lady travel
> **Edited:** historical comparisons to the travel of previous first ladies

Caparisons are decorative adornments worn by horses; the author meant *comparisons*. *Former first lady travel* is both awkward and ambiguous: Does *former* denote *former travel* or travel by *former first ladies*, which would imply travel after their husbands weren't president any more?

As published, it read, "comparisons to the solo travel of previous first ladies," which was even better than my edited version.

Six Words Shorter

> are able to perform the multitude of tasks required to maintain
> a high level of homeland defense while at the same time stand-
> ing ready

To say the same thing with fewer words, I replaced *are able to* with *can*, and I deleted *at the same time*.

> can perform the multitude of tasks required to maintain a high
> level of homeland defense while standing ready

No Manners

Usually I shorten references to things that are done in a manner or on a basis or in nature—for example, *in a cost-effective manner* is a long way of writing *cost-effectively*. Things considered *on a case-by-case basis* get considered *case by case*. Things that are *complicated in nature* are just *complicated*. These are all real examples I've seen, and those extra words didn't help communication at all.

Humanitarian Editing

The adjective *humanitarian* means "concerned with or seeking to promote human welfare," according to the *Oxford Dictionary*, which offers a secondary meaning of involving "widespread human suffering, especially [requiring] large-scale provision of aid." Call me a curmudgeon (and you'd probably be right), but I suspect that this second definition was added to accommodate a ghastly misuse of the word *humanitarian*, given in two examples by the *Oxford Dictionary*: "humanitarian crisis" and "humanitarian disaster." This makes *humanitarian* into what William Safire called a Janus word: one with opposite meanings—in this case, (1) benefiting humanity and (2) horrible for humanity. I checked five other dictionaries, and none of them gave the second meaning of something horrible, though I daresay some of them will eventually.

In one article I edited, I changed *humanitarian crises* to *crises requiring humanitarian response*. Yes, it's twice as long, but shorter isn't always better. Please do the same. If you see *humanitarian crisis* or *humanitarian disaster*, kill it with a stick and replace it with *crisis requiring humanitarian response* or *disaster requiring humanitarian response*, as appropriate. A curmudgeon will thank you.

Implant This

database design and implantation experience

Implantation should have been *implementation*. *Implant* is on my list of bad words to search for when editing a document (see "Homophones and Other Words That Get Mixed Up" in chapter seven, "A Few Tips"). It's surprising how often *implant* turns up where it doesn't belong. I found it five times in a company's list of things it offered via a General Services Administration schedule.

Obstacles to Communication: The Wrong Word?

poses underestimated obstacles

I queried this: Who underestimated them? Should it say *unexpected*?

The final version was thoroughly rewritten and mentioned implicit obstacles.

NASA Who?

NASA is one of those names that is commonly known, and in aerospace publications I expect that the readers would know what it is. What about the writers? In one technical document I edited, I had to change National Aerospace and Space Administration to the correct name, National Aeronautics and Space Administration.

Sue of Multimethodology

A silly bibliographic entry I came across: "The sue of multi-methodology in Practice – Results of a Survey of Practioners." The correct title was "The Use of Multimethodology in Practice—Results of a Survey of Practitioners." I don't know why the author capitalized nouns in the subtitle but not the title. Blame it on Sue.

Wrong Adjective? *Former*

taken up by former National Security Advisor Tom Donilon

This indicates something taken up by Donilon after he was National Security Advisor (the former advisor took it up). If he acted while National Security Advisor, it should read, "taken up by Tom Donilon when he was National Security Advisor." The published version had the latter wording.

Myanmar: The Formal Name

In editing a piece about Burma, I asked whether the name *Myanmar* should be used instead of Burma, or at least mentioned in the copy. The country is commonly known as Burma, but its official name is Myanmar. I guess the answer was no, because the name *Myanmar* was not in the published document.

Capital Offenses

I had to correct all these typos in assorted documents: EXPEDITONARY, EXPOLITATION, INLCUDE, PARAGRAPSH, REQUIRMENT, OFFICAL, and maybe a hundred others. Why? Because a Microsoft Word default setting under Proofing is "Ignore words in UPPERCASE." When the writers ran a spell-check, Word sped right past these typos.

Nonidiomatic Phrasing

Original: other nations take efforts to make it easier
Edited: other nations work to make it easier

"Take effort" is not idiomatic English. I could have changed *take* to *make*, but I felt that having *make* twice in the sentence and so close together sounded awkward, which is why I changed *take efforts* to *work*.

View Program

View intern program

This was a hyperlink. It sounded as if clicking on it would take you to a video on YouTube. Actually it led to a document describing the program; it didn't let you actually see the program, so I added the word *description* to the end.

Odd Commas and a Lonely Quotation Mark

Murray Hiebert wrote: China, clearly recognizes the importance of courting the leader of Thailand. Beijing has invited Yingluck to visit China twice between now and mid-September. ..."

This clearly was wrong: There was an ending quotation mark but no beginning quote mark. I verify every quotation I can, and when I looked up this one I found out what was going on. For one thing, the quotation had two authors, and only one was named. I broke up the quote because the original subject of the first sentence was omitted, leaving a stray comma after what is now grammatically the subject, *China*, and because the *now* in the quotation was seven weeks previous. Here's the edited version.

> Murray Hiebert and Noelan Arbis wrote that China "clearly recognizes the importance of courting the leader of Thailand," having "invited Yingluck to visit China twice between" early August "and mid-September. ..."

Near Editing

> **Original:** the near constant challenge
> **Edited:** the nearly constant challenge

Maybe this is another curmudgeonly complaint, but I don't like the sound of *near* as an adverb. Some would edit that phrase with a hyphen (near-constant), but it still sounds bad to me. *Nearly* not only has a grammatical pedigree, but it also doesn't need the hyphen, because it's an adverb that ends in *-ly*.

The same editing applies to "near-real-time" data (for example): That's an awkward modifying phrase requiring two hyphens, and if we need to talk about real-time anything as opposed to, perhaps, unreal time or fake time, the adverb *nearly* does the job better. *Almost* would work, too.

An Awfully Long Modifying Phrase

> the USAF-People's Liberation Army Air Force (PLAAF) mil-to-mil relationship is immature

You had to get a long way into this phrasing to find out the subject of the sentence: *relationship*. The modifying phrase *mil-to-mil* could cause readers to hesitate, if not stumble, so I spelled it out. *USAF* (U.S. Air Force) was spelled out earlier in the article. In the edited version, the preposition *between* alerts readers that the parties to the relationship will be named next and that what follows is a modifying phrase. This was my solution.

> the military-to-military relationship between the USAF and the People's Liberation Army Air Force (PLAAF) is immature

Often you will find more than one satisfactory editing solution to awkward wording. Here's another:

> the USAF and the People's Liberation Army Air Force (PLAAF) have an immature military-to-military relationship

Plagiarism Tip-Off

> killing including the mission's chief, <u>Hédi Annabi</u>

What was wrong with this, besides the lack of an object for the verb *killing*? That underlined text had a hyperlink to a Wikipedia page about Hédi Annabi. That's often a sign that the writer copied text out of Wikipedia, including hyperlinks to other Wikipedia pages. When I see that warning sign, I start scrutinizing the text for possible plagiarism. In this case, not only was the text copied, it was mangled. Here's the text I found on the Wikipedia page "2010 Haiti Earthquake":

> killing many, including the Mission's Chief, Hédi Annabi.

This text from the same article had another Wikipedia link, on the words *Médecins sans Frontières*, but without the underlining or blue text:

> The earthquake severely damaged the three Médecins sans Frontières (doctors without borders) medical facilities around Port-au-Prince, causing one to collapse completely

If you become suspicious and you are using a newer version of Microsoft Word, you can choose to show all the hyperlinks. Look under "More commands," "Advanced," "Show document content," and check the box for "Show field codes instead of their values." Here's the same text displayed that way:

> The earthquake severely damaged the { HYPERLINK
> http://en.wikipedia.org/wiki/M%C3%A9decins_Sans_
> Fronti%C3%A8res \o "Médecins sans Frontières" } three
> Médecins sans Frontières (doctors without borders) medical facil-
> ities around Port-au-Prince, causing one to collapse completely

And here's the text from the Wikipedia page.

> The quake affected the three Médecins Sans Frontières (Doctors
> Without Borders) medical facilities around Port-au-Prince, caus-
> ing one to collapse completely

The plagiarist changed one word and improperly made *Doctors Without Borders* lowercase. It's a bungled burglary, but it's still stealing.

Starting a Quote Partway Through

> stated that "… the department has not developed guidance"

Words Into Type explains that ellipsis points are not usually needed at the beginning of an excerpted quotation: "Points of ellipsis at the beginning of an excerpt starting in mid-sentence merely emphasize a fact already marked by the small letter for the first word, but in some scholarly and technical works, this emphasis is desirable."[215] In this case, I got rid of the ellipsis points.

Verify the Quote, the Source, Anything You Can

> The 2009 Department of Defense review of force protec-
> tion measures, "*Protecting the Force: Lessons Learned from Fort
> Hood*," recommended actions to "significantly improve the
> Department's ability to mitigate internal threats, ensure force pro-
> tection, enable emergency response, and provide care for victims
> and families."

I had a PDF of the cited report (and could have downloaded one if need be). I verified that it was published in 2010, not 2009, and that

Learned wasn't part of the subtitle, which was *Lessons from Fort Hood*. And I searched the electronic copy of the report but could not find the quotation. So I turned to Google and found what was apparently the correct source, which I passed on to the writers: This quote appears to be not from *Protecting the Force* but from a Secretary of Defense memo describing the results of the follow-on review.

A Makeover for a Defense Department Chief

a re-fashioned and strengthened Department of Defense Chief Information Officer (DOD CIO) was created to harmonize evolving business practices

I imagined God breathing life into this creation, as in Michelangelo's painting of God touching Adam. This sentence mentions evolution, too. This was the Pentagon, so we know that there wasn't any intelligent design involved. I just queried this whole creation story: "The officer is a person, correct? Refashioned, etc.? Or has the job or position or office been refashioned, strengthened, and created?"

In this case, I was able to look at the final published document, in which *Officer* had been changed to *Office*.

Keep Titles as Written, If They Are Written Correctly

The same piece above referred to a Deputy CIO for "Command Control Communications Computers (C4) Information and Integration Capabilities." I didn't have a list of Defense Department Deputy Chief Information Officers to check against, so I queried this, too: "Are there no commas in this title?" The Pentagon is not a paragon of good grammar, but it's usually not *that* bad. The final publication had sprouted four commas in the title, which was a relief: "Command, Control, Communications, and Computers (C4), Information and Integration Capabilities."

Speaking of Defense Department titles, there's the Assistant Secretary of Defense for Homeland Defense & Americas' Security

Affairs. That's the real title, with plural *Americas* followed by an apostrophe. My hunch is that somebody got it wrong when the title was devised, and then it was too late to change it. In plain English (which I admit, is not a strong suit at the Pentagon—there's a reason that military people call the place the Puzzle Palace), when referring to North and South America, we call them "the Americas," not just "Americas," so if this assistant secretary was being charged with the security affairs of the Americas, there should have been a *the* in the title. My guess: It was supposed to be *America's* but somebody put the apostrophe in the wrong place and it remained there.

The Center Is Down There

fusion centers have become epicenters of information sharing

An epicenter is the point above the center, such as the point on the surface of the Earth above the center of an earthquake. I deleted *epi*. Fusion centers are the centers; they are not above the centers. However, as a *Writer's Digest* editor helpfully pointed out, my editing was not a total success: I ended up with the word *centers* twice, and only three words apart. Changing *epicenters* to *hubs* would have been a better idea.

Catastrophe Focus Groups?

[The researchers] obtained feedback directly from the emergency response community regarding their current missions, the capabilities available to fulfill those missions, and existing constraints and issues that affect capability to successfully respond to a catastrophic incident through a series of focus groups, a workshop, and other data gathering opportunities.

The original sounded as if focus groups and a workshop were part of the response to a catastrophe. (I also queried whether a catastrophic incident is the same as a catastrophe.) Here's the edited version, in which the focus groups, etc., are aligned with feedback (you know, that screeching noise that a microphone produces sometimes?).

[The researchers] obtained feedback directly from the emergency response community—through a series of focus groups, a workshop, and other data-gathering opportunities—regarding their current missions, the capabilities available to fulfill those missions, and existing constraints and issues that affect capability to successfully respond to a catastrophic incident.

Ambiguity! En Garde!

Be on guard against ambiguity. The books *Red Tape Holds Up New Bridge* and *Squad Helps Dog Bite Victim*, both from the *Columbia Journalism Review*, have loads of entertaining examples. This one (from my own experience, not from the books) wasn't funny, just confusing.

> To streamline evaluation and document review tasks

Is *document* here a verb or noun? To streamline tasks involving document review and evaluation, or to streamline evaluation and to document the review tasks?

The published version read, "To streamline evaluation and to document review tasks …"

Check Repeated Information

One item on my copy-editing checklist (see chapter nine, "The Editor's Tools") is "Check repeated information." One document I was editing referred to an organization's Partner Exercise Division. In another place it was the Partner Exercise Branch. This was another question for the author: Is it Division or Branch?

Focus Responsibly

> the multi-nation faculty is responsible for contributing to a book that represents the focus of the key lessons learned

This had several faults, none of them very big. *Multination* is one word in *Merriam-Webster's Collegiate Dictionary*, 10th edition. Saying that the "faculty is responsible for contributing to a book" sounds as if the job isn't finished, but in fact the book had already been published. And did the book represent the focus, whatever that means? No, it presented the lessons learned (I knew, because I edited that book). So here is the edited text after several small improvements.

> the multination faculty was responsible for contributing to a book that presents the key lessons learned

The Untied States

The Untied States: Isn't that what happened during the Civil War? I see that typo so often that it's on my list of bad words to search for in every document that might mention the *United* States. Other common variants are *Unites States* and *United Sates*, and a spell-check might not notice anything wrong with them.

Buzzword Bingo

> the Army must be prepared to prevent, shape, and win

There were no objects for those verbs. They were all used as if they were intransitive. *Win* can be intransitive: We have to win! But not *prevent* or *shape*: We have to prevent! We have to shape! I really think that some writers simply string buzzwords together and hope that the sum of the parts will have some meaning. All I could do was query this: Prevent and shape what?

Dollars, Dollars

One document mentioned the "F-35 Lightening II," an airplane. (It should read *Lightning*— the typo reminds me of the engineering credo "add more lightness," attributed to Gordon Hooton.) It cited some sky-high numbers: $1.1 trillion dollars and $1.5 trillion dollars for the whole program. A trillion here, a trillion there, and pretty soon you're talking about real money.* But the numbers were redundant. You don't need a dollar sign *and* the word *dollars.*

There They Go Again

> A given defense force commander is responsible for the safety and security of their base, including the base's integrity, physical assets, civilian support, active duty personnel, and their dependents. In order to successfully fulfill these responsibilities, they're constantly challenged.

Since a commander may be a man or a woman, the writer referred to the commander as *they.* A lot of writers and editors say that using a plural pronoun that way is okay and has a long history. I think there's always a better way. But there's more to this case. The second sentence was confusing because the first sentence was loaded with plural nouns: *assets, personnel, dependents.* And "they" are constantly challenged. So I got rid of the plural pronouns.

> A given defense force commander is responsible for the safety and security of the base, including the base's integrity, physical assets, civilian support, active-duty personnel, and their dependents. To successfully fulfill these responsibilities, the commander is constantly challenged.

I also should have deleted *given,* which in this case means "specified." *Any* defense force commander would be challenged.

See Where the Link Leads

Check every hyperlink to verify that it works and that it leads where the text says it does.

---

* Senator Everett Dirksen is famously quoted as saying, "A billion here, a billion there, pretty soon, you're talking real money." (He was being sarcastic about federal spending.)

As FEMA's Administrator Craig Fugate pointed out in his "all hands" presentation "Planning for the Whole Community" in April 2011, "We don't plan for easy in FEMA … we plan for real."

This text had a hyperlink, but it didn't lead to Fugate's "all hands" presentation. It linked to an April 2011 briefing apparently from Marcie Roth, director of the FEMA Office of Disability Integration and Coordination; the briefing contained the Fugate quote, dated March 2010. Here's the corrected text.

As FEMA's Administrator Craig Fugate pointed out in March 2010, "We don't plan for easy in FEMA … we plan for real."

From … To

A lot of writers use the construction *from … to*, with a range of things exemplified by their first and last items, as in the cliché *from soup to nuts* (presuming those to be the first and last courses of a big meal, something I find questionable). Some of those constructions (the cliché is an example) don't necessarily indicate two ends of a spectrum. Worse, some writers seem to define the beginning of a spectrum and forget to end it. Maybe that happened here.

from innovating new technologies to detect chemical and biological threats

Or maybe not. Is this supposed to be a range, with *innovating* at one end and *detecting* (not *detect*) at the other? Or are these technologies to detect threats, in which case what is coming *from* them? Another author query.

The published version:

This assistance ranges from innovating new technologies to detecting chemical and biological threats for force protection

The Future May Be the Past

A document dated May said that an institute would hold two reviews: one in February and one in April. At face value, this would imply reviews taking place the following year. But maybe this document was drafted in January and nobody updated the tense. I queried the author, asking that the text be changed if the reviews had already taken place.

My hunch was right, and the published document said that the institute had "held two reviews."

The Party of the First Part Shall Be Known in This Contract as the Party of the First Part

If you know that scene from the Marx Brothers' film *A Night at the Opera*, you know what comes next: Groucho and Chico tear out the parts of the contract Chico doesn't like, most of them redundantly identifying the party of the first part, the party of the second part, and so on. By the time Groucho and Chico get to tearing out the party of the ninth part, there's almost nothing left of the contract. "Yeah, it's-a too long, anyhow," as Chico said. I did something like that with this:

> Swim lane methodology is best suited to "above the factory floor" or administrative processes. Swim lane mapping methodology takes its name from a swimming pool with its lanes. Each swimmer stays in their assigned lane throughout the race. Similarly, in the swim lanes map, each individual or functionary has an assigned lane.

Okay, we get it. We know what swim lanes look like. Here it is after I tore out the parts I didn't like.

> Swim lane methodology is best suited to "above the factory floor" or administrative processes. Each individual or functionary has an assigned lane.

Here's an example of tautology* that sounds like it could have been in the Marx Brothers' contract.

> The Defense Security Service's (DSS) Center for Development
> of Security Excellence (CDSE) has the mission to provide the
> Department of Defense with a security center of excellence

This Didn't Really Help

Here are a few edits I made that didn't do the job.

> **Original:** protect these first responders with personnel protective
> equipment
> **Edited:** equip these first responders with personal protective
> equipment

I thought that to *protect* them with protective equipment was redundant, and I changed it to *equipping* them with equipment. Although *provide* is a bit vague and overused, it might have been the better substitute for *equip* in this case.

■■■■■

"Modeling scenarios predict a serious chemical disaster," stated one article. It sounds as if scientists had concluded that one was imminent. The sentence continued, however: "Modeling scenarios predict a serious chemical disaster could result in hundreds to a few thousand casualties …" Readers had to get to the eighth word before learning that the scenarios predicted the possible results of a disaster. I added *that* after *predict*: "Modeling scenarios predict that a serious chemical disaster could result in hundreds to a few thousand casualties …"

So far, so good. But "hundreds to a few thousand casualties"? That slipped right by me. I should have changed it to something like "casualties—anywhere from hundreds to a few thousand."

---

* "Needless repetition of an idea," according to *Merriam-Webster's Collegiate Dictionary*, 10th edition.

Don't Try This at Home, Kids

One thing I've been taught in editorial training is not to commit smart-aleck remarks to paper (or to comments embedded in a document file). The person reading them may not know they're supposed to be funny or may know it and not agree. Still, now and then Mr. Hyde displaces Dr. Jekyll.

> the lead planner was lost.

"Killed?" I asked. "Missing? Fired? Retired? Reassigned? Crash-landed on a mysterious island?" The phrase needed clarification, but maybe I should have stopped after *reassigned*.

■■■■■

> for use by public and private school systems in planning, training and responding to food contamination events

I changed it to this.

> for use by public and private school systems in planning for, training for, and responding to food contamination events

And I helpfully pointed out, "If they are planning food contamination events, that should be the headline."

■■■■■

> the cost figures ... reported by the Air Force and Army are remarkably uniform for each Service

My comment wasn't really smart-alecky, just a pun: That's because they are uniformed Services. I'm sure the writers are still laughing about that one!

■■■■■

[a] presentation and generation model ... for possible implantation

"Implementation?" I asked. "or are they supposed to stick it someplace?" That was a reasonable question, actually. *Implant* is also in my list of bad words to search for in any document that might (or *should*) contain the word *implement*.

11

Ones That Got Away

This chapter presents some dumb mistakes that have appeared in print—what one writer called "Steve's Hall of Shame." They aren't my personal mistakes; I collected them for use in editing classes. A few of them need no explanation, but if there's any doubt as to how they could have been caught, I'll refer to the editorial checklist or another of the editor's tools.

For fun or practice, try to figure out the problem with each clipping before reading the explanation.

Van driver recovering from fatal Stafford crash

Fredericksburg, Virginia, *Free Lance–Star*

This sounds like a zombie story. Probably someone else died and the driver was injured, but the headline sounds weird. Be on the lookout for text with possible double meanings.

■■■■■

Kids gets clothing, vaccines for school

Fredericksburg, Virginia, *Free Lance–Star*

I don't mean to pick on the *Free Lance–Star*. It's published a lot of my writing. But it's my local paper, so it's a major supplier to Steve's Hall of Shame. I've long recommended running a spelling and grammar check even on headlines. If a copy editor is reading too fast to notice something wrong with "Kids gets," at least the word processor's grammar check should pause when it comes to that.

ALEX BRANDON / ASSOCIATED PRESS

Nationals second baseman Anthony Rendon (6) bobbles the ball but still get records Buster Posey's out Tuesday.

Fredericksburg, Virginia, *Free Lance–Star*

This caption is messed up in two ways. First of all, it identifies a player by his number, 6, but the number isn't visible in the photo, although from the picture, you can deduce that the player who isn't number 28 must be number 6. Also, he's clearly wearing a Nationals uniform. But what does "get records Buster Posey's out" mean? "Buster Posey" is right—Buster is his first name, or at least his nickname. Maybe it originally said "records-buster" (Posey has set records) or even "records-buster Buster Posey," and somebody tried to improve it. Always make sure the caption matches the picture and makes sense.

Bombs still victim of roadside bombs

Fredericksburg, Virginia, *Free Lance–Star*

It's so sad when bombs get hurt, isn't it? I can't imagine a way to read this headline so that it makes sense. The story, from 2008, was about continuing violence in Iraq. Maybe somebody was rewriting the headline and got interrupted.

■■■■■

A promising mission field

Despite being ravaged by the sexual revolution, a Catholic theologian says American youths hunger for the truth.

By FRANCIS X. ROCCA
Catholic News Service

VATICAN CITY — In sexual morality, family life and education, the Baby Boom generation ushered in a series of cultural changes that ticipating in the plenary assembly of the Pontifical Council for Culture, which met in early February to address the theme of "emerg-

Arlington, Virginia, *Catholic Herald*

The subheading says that the theologian pictured was ravaged by the sexual revolution. The story does not. A comma after *says* would have corrected the meaning. Better yet would have been to put the attribution at the end: "Despite being ravaged by the sexual revolution,

American youths still hunger for the truth, a Catholic theologian says."
The *Catholic Herald* is generally a well-edited paper (editor Laura
Moyer, formerly of the *Free Lance–Star*, agrees). Unlike the *Free Lance–
Star*, it rarely provides material for Steve's Hall of Shame. Maybe if it
came out daily …

■■■■■

Eric L. Chase
To Punish and Deter Grevious Misconduct in War

The Washington Post

■■■■■

White trucker dies after defending black fiend

Fredericksburg, Virginia, *Free Lance–Star*

This item from 2000 described a white man defending a black, uh,
friend from a racial incident in Texas. Now who will protect him from
the slur in the headline? A spelling and grammar check wouldn't have
caught this. The only defense is careful reading, though coffee helps, too.

ASSOCIATED PRESS

Vannever Bush in 1947

The Washington Post

Vannevar is hard to spell. We'll help you out with a picture of the nameplate on his desk. As the editorial checklist says, "Check repeated information."

■■■■■

SUNDAY, SEPTEMBER 31, 1997

Fredericksburg, Virginia, *Free Lance–Star*

Thirty days hath September, except in leap year, when it has thirty-one, and February is just too hard to remember. Aside from memorizing the rhyme about how many days are in each month, it's a good idea to check a calendar to see, for example, whether September 31 is truly on a Sunday. It wasn't on the calendar at all! I took the calendar back for a refund.

■■■■■

Passenger groups at odds on rail line

By Kathleen Cannon
BCT staff writer

Which one to believe?

Two railroad passenger groups — one based in Philadelphia, the other in Newark — have different slants on NJ Transit's plan to construct a $450 light rail system linking Camden to Trenton along the Delaware River.

Jersey association board member who says he left that group two years ago because it gave short shrift to southern New Jersey.

"I believe that that organization is just interested in acting as a cheerleader for NJT in South Jersey ... to gain favor for projects they're concerned with in North Jersey," Nigro said yesterday.

Bowen, of Hoboken, dismissed Nigro's criticism. He said his group advocates for mass transit on behalf of the entire state, as far

Burlington County (New Jersey) *Times*

I've seen this error so many times that it's no longer funny to me. An important word—probably *million*—was left out after *$450* in the second paragraph of this article. Always check numbers to see whether they are at least plausible.

Program celebrates Black History Month

Jane Henderson, past president of the Stafford Historical Society, and Janet Payne, coordinating teacher for fine arts in Stafford County public schools, will be the featured speakers in a program celebrating Black History Month.

Henderson will present a program on the area's stone quarries—how they operated, how stones were transported by water, and where the stones are still being used today.

Payne will discuss the works of artist Palmer Hayden, who spent his boyhood years in Stafford County.

The program, sponsored by the Stafford branch of the National Asso-

The club meets the third Friday of each month at the Lake of the Woods clubhouse.

Writers gather to form local club

A group of Fredericksburg-area writers are gathering next week to establish a local chapter of the Virginia Writers Club.

The meeting, which is open to the public, will be held at the Salem Church Library on Thursday, Feb. 18, at 2:30 p.m.

Author Joanne Pizarro of Igloo Publishing is the featured speaker.

Anyone needing more information should call Betty Marcum at 898-8627.

Fredericksburg, Virginia, *Free Lance–Star*

What's wrong with the writers' club announcement? The dateline at the top of the paper says, "Tuesday, February 17." The meeting is listed for "next week," on "Thursday, Feb. 18." Not only would that not be the following week, but if Tuesday is February 17, Thursday can't be February 18. February sure is a crazy month, calendar-wise.

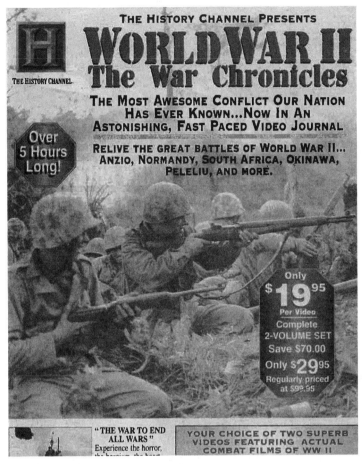

History Channel ad

It's good for copy editors to have a general knowledge of history, geography, science—everything we learned in high school but may have forgotten. For that matter, it's a good idea for History Channel ad writers to have a general knowledge of history. "The war to end all wars" was a slogan applied to World War I, not World War II, and there were no battles in South Africa during World War II. North Africa, yes. And who would want to "relive" these battles, anyway?

Adoption reforms frought with peril

The Washington Post

Headline writing is fraught with peril, too.

■■■■■

Rugged 4.5-Mile Course Built for Mountain Bikers

By Patricia Davis
Washington Post Staff Writer

The narrow dirt trail snakes through some of Northern Virginia's most scenic and rugged terrain, a 4.5-mile obstacle course with hills to climb, creeks to cross and logs to hurtle.

The Washington Post

The bikers could hurdle (leap over) the logs as they go hurtling (racing) through the woods. This is another case where the spelling and grammar check won't save the writer. The only defense is careful reading and, if there's any doubt about a word's meaning, a handy dictionary.

Area may be shook by tourist boom

Washington Times

Maybe it will. The boom may leave it all shook up. A spelling and grammar check could have saved the headline.

■■■■■

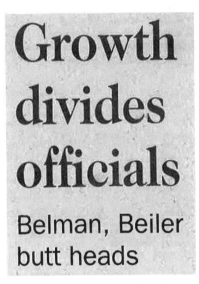

Growth divides officials

Belman, Beiler butt heads

Fredericksburg, Virginia, *Free Lance–Star*

And Beavis, too. Technically there's nothing wrong with this. At best, it's an unhappy turn of phrase. At worst, it's an opportunity to insult the officials. All it takes is one accidental keystroke to make the last two words into one.

Fredericksburg, Virginia, *Free Lance–Star*

Orang County, Virginia. How did they manage to fit the whole word *Westmoreland* if there isn't room for *Orange* or *Essex*? More times than I can remember, I've seen text that didn't fit into text boxes or table cells, with words lopped off or split incorrectly, as with "Newpor t" in the lower right corner of this clip. It's essential to actually read graphics, maps, and tables to find things that could go wrong in layout.

The traffic problems
The answer is allusive

New super highways barely keep pace
with the increased number of motor vehicles.

By Greg Ovechka

Before school gets out for the summer, why don't we open our textbook *New Jersey: The Garden State* and turn to Chapter 23 — "The Traffic Problem in New Jersey."

"One ironic characteristic of present-day life in New Jersey is that," the authors tell us, "in an age of supersonic speed and space travel, it is becoming increasingly difficult to move a few miles on the ground from one population center to another. The modern motor car, with all its great speed and comfort, has not been an unmixed blessing in tiny, crowded New Jersey.

"Major additions to the highway system are planned or under construction, including a rapid-transit system serving the Philadelphia-Camden metropolitan area.

"No one can say now to what extent these schemes (and others along the same lines) will prove feasible. It is clear, however, that some new means of public transportation will have to be provided to serve the vast numbers of commuters who make their home in New Jersey. Essentially the same problem exists today in many other parts of the United States, but in few places is it as acute or far-reaching as in the sections of New Jersey which form part of the greatest metropolitan area in the nation."

And now for your quiz: take out a pencil, open you blue book and answer the follow-

Cape May-Lewes Ferry provides needed transportation between lower Delaware and Garden State Parkway users.

New Jersey Success

This is a three-part test, so open you blue book. Actually, before you open *your* blue book, open your dictionary and look up *allusive* and *elusive*, especially if you think the ferry provides transportation between Delaware and Garden State Parkway users (see the caption). If good writing and editing equal success, they missed the boat this time.

South Oaks (Spotsylvania, Virginia) Homeowners Association

Guess we'll have to tear down that garage. And you're wondering what *ebris* is? This is unsightly, all right.

■■■■■

The water supply authority began acquiring land for the reservoir in 1970, purchasing 1,278 acres of woods, farmland and wetlands just north of Interstate 195 and south of Peskin Road and Southard Avenue. The reservoir will cover 740 acres — more than one square mile — and will be contained by a 4,500-foot-long damn built of sand and clay dredged from the site.

Asbury Park (New Jersey) *Press*

The world's longest curse word.

■■■■■

Stuff of which dreams are made on

Fredericksburg, Virginia, *Free Lance–Star*

This headline writer was no Shakespeare: There are too many prepositions here. How Shakespeare put it in *The Tempest* was "We are such stuff/As dreams are made on." If you want a modern paraphrase, "We are made of the stuff of which dreams are màde."

SPRING LAKE TRAGEDY

Photo by Georgine Stoner/*HERALD*

Chief Ron Shelton, of the U.S. Coast Guard Shark River Station, draws a diagram in the sand for Sgt. Robert Brophy, a diver for the Spring Lake/Spring Lake Heights Special Emergency Response Team, to detail the best area of underwater search for Ismael Menendez, Elizabeth. Menendez, 19, disappeared in the surf off the Union Avenue beachfront in Spring Lake Sunday and is presumed drowned by authorities. Also involved in rescue efforts at the scene were: (l-r) Spring Lake Assistant Emergency Management Coordinator Bill Watson, and firemen Bill Newman and Bill Brahn.

Asbury Park (New Jersey) *Press*

It was the authorities who drowned her? One way that the second sentence could have been fixed would be to split it into two: "Menendez, 19, disappeared in the surf off the Union Avenue beachfront in Spring Lake Sunday. Authorities presume that she drowned."

This shoe
is on display

Ask
salesperson
for mate

Paper in a shoe in a store

This is what I call the false economy of omitting small words. Adding *its* in front of *mate* would save embarrassment for the person who thinks that the store offers a matchmaking service.

■ ■ ■ ■ ■

REZA MARVASHTI / THE FREE LANCE-STAR

Robert J. Dickenson III, a member of Old Colony Council's Troop 515 from Massachusetts, makes his way up the final leg of the Army's climbing wall. The wall is at the entrance to the Army Adventure area at the 2001 National Scout Jamboree.

Military mines jamboree

By PAMELA GOULD
THE FREE LANCE-STAR

Gather 32,820 young men with a talent for teamwork, a sense of adventure and an appreciation for discipline and you've got a military recruiter's dream.

Unabashedly, members of the Army, Navy, Air Force, Coast Guard and Marine Corps admit the 13- to 18-year-olds assembled for 10 days at Fort A.P. Hill for the National Scout Jamboree are tailor-made to fill their ranks.

"One of the reasons we're doing this," said Senior Master Sgt. David Kinsey of the Virginia Air National Guard, "is we saw very fertile ground of young men who like to

wear a uniform and like to achieve rank."

Granted, most are much too young to make a formal commitment, but that doesn't mean the officers can't take the opportunity to show off what their services offer.

Like how it feels to get behind the controls of an Air Force F-16 fighter jet.

Or what the Army's Apache attack helicopters look like up close.

Or that the Marine Corps is affiliated with NASCAR and a team that runs a Chevrolet Monte Carlo in the Busch Grand National series.

See MILITARY, Page A8

REZA MARVASHTI / THE FREE LANCE-STAR

'Wow,' says Ben Owen (left) as his friend Justin handles an unloaded, nonfunctional M-16 automatic rifle with grenade launcher.

Fredericksburg, Virginia, *Free Lance–Star*

Exactly what is the military doing at the Boy Scout jamboree? It sounds as if the Army is laying a minefield. Here a word with two meanings makes a minefield for the reader.

Artist sheds light on deep wreck: Edmund Fitzgerald

'Does anyone know where the love of God goes when the waves turn the minutes to hours?'
—**Gordon Lightfoot, "The Wreck of the Edmund Fitzgerald"**

RICHARD SULLIVAN never intended to become an authority on a famous shipwreck, it just worked out that way.

But Sullivan, a Colonial Beach artist and illustrator, doesn't pick up his pens and brushes until he knows his subject, and he spent months constructing his masterpiece: a scale model of the largest and most famous shipwreck ever on the Great Lakes—the Edmund Fitzgerald.

His chillingly realistic paintings and a 4-foot diorama of the stricken ship, built up from paper, are currently displayed at the Marquette Maritime Museum in Michigan.

Sullivan (no relation) contacted me recently after seeing a column I had written some time ago about the sinking of the Titanic.

ARMCHAIR ADVENTURES

Paul Sullivan

Although I had heard of the Fitzgerald sinking, I really knew nothing about it. Sullivan took care of that problem. After all, those of us who grow up along the mid-Atlantic are but dimly aware of the Great Lakes and the entire culture surrounding them.

But Richard Sullivan grew up in that environment. Raised in Milwaukee, the son of a veteran Lakes shipmaster, he signed on to a freighter plying those inland waters as a young man.

Little did he know then that, many years later, he would be the official artist for the U.S. Coast Guard inquiry into the most famous Lakes shipwreck of them all.

In the lore of the vast inland lakes, he said, "They call the sinking of the Fitzgerald the 'Titanic' of the Great Lakes." Of the more than 6,000 wrecks on the Great Lakes, Sullivan said the 1975 loss of the mammoth ore carrier continues to intrigue seafarers and the public.

PAUL SULLIVAN

Artist Richard Sullivan of Colonial Beach (above) created this model of the Edmund Fitzgerald, a mammoth ore carrier that sank in 1975. It's been called the 'Titanic' of the Great Lakes. His painting (top) depicts the sunken ship.

Fredericksburg, Virginia, *Free Lance–Star*

That caption isn't shipshape. You don't have to be nautically minded to see that the "model of the Edmund Fitzgerald, a mammoth ore carrier," looks nothing like the *Edmund Fitzgerald* pictured at the top of the page. In fact, it looks like the Confederate submarine *Hunley*.

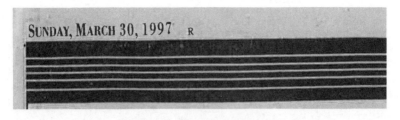

SUNDAY, MARCH 30, 1997   R

Just Plain Dumb

*A Seasonal Homage to Bad Ideas, Bonehead Moves
And Other Famous Foolishness*

By Michael Farquhar
Washington Post Staff Writer

his just in: There are wide-

This week we celebrate famous foolishnesses. Why? Because today is April 1, an appropriate time to delight in others' silly mistakes.

The Washington Post

Is this an April Fool's joke? The dateline says March 30, but the text says, "Today is April 1." Maybe the writer expected the piece to be published on April 1. Check repeated information.

■ ■ ■ ■ ■

FOCUS ON FIRE SAFETY
Fireworks and
Outdoor Cooking Fire Safety

U.S. Fire Administration website

The heading makes you think the article is about using fireworks while cooking, and I expected to see firecrackers on the grill alongside the burgers and hot dogs. However, it was two separate safety topics combined in one article.

192 ■ ▪ The Editor's Companion

The island's 9-hole golf course has become more difficult to reach now that daily fairy service has been discontinued.

Fredericksburg, Virginia, *Free Lance–Star*

Tinker Bell no longer flies to the island every day. But maybe if we wish really hard, the caption writer will be more careful and silly typos will be discontinued. But then who would supply Steve's Hall of Shame?

come to a stop. Some systems, such as the Siemens intermittent ATC system (called ZUB) take the extra step of creating a record of the incident, which subsequently can be used for investigative and training enforcement.

Amtrak recently tested one of these systems, Union Switch & Signal's intermittent cab signaling system, along a section of the Northeast Corridor. Called ACSES, it provides civil and temporary

Mass Transit

Here's another instance where a little geographical knowledge can help an editor spot errors. Is Redondo Beach (on the destination sign of this train) in Illinois (as the caption says)? No, it's in California.

Frontline

Exercise vigilance—run a spell-check.

■ ■ ■ ■ ■

The Korea Herald

Monday, December 16, 2002

Search [   ] 🔍

◁ᵕᵖ Announcement
- 2003 Àꟼ› °ü¼Áõ¿ª
  ¿ª»¢'ᴮÉ ż'æ
- The 35th Annual Korean
  Folk Arts Festival For
  Foreigners

English Update
»¢¼ª, ±'Ấ¦™¼°, Annie's
MailboxÀÇ °ø¿ª¹× µè±â
±â´É°ú
¼ÇÀü¿µ¹/¼Ä×¼°Æ®¿ᵃÄꟼ°

I like that English update.

In Cooporation with <u>ISI Training Center</u>

An advertisement on the Chameleon Associates website

These heavily armed men appear to be cooperatively guarding the coop.

■■■■■

Lampson on NASA short list

$2.1 million offered for suspect on most-wanted list —
Mexican officials say they have arrested one of their most-wanted drug

Houston Chronicle

Lampson was on the short list to be the NASA administrator. Unfortunately the headline seems to have gotten pinned to a story about someone else on a different list.

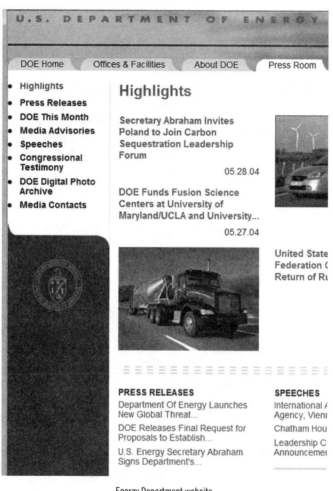

Energy Department website

Look at the first press release title. The structure of the website appears to truncate headlines with regard to length, not with regard to whether the result makes sense. In this case, we can hope that the Energy Department was not launching a global threat.

The correct name, appearing just above the main headline, is Coral Gables. It appears that a hasty headline writer hit the *G* key too many times.

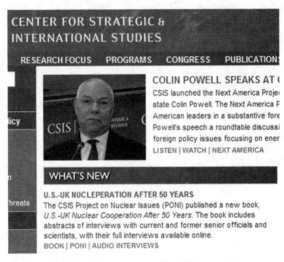

Center for Strategic and International Studies website

After fifty years, the U.S. and UK finally got nucleperation. I hope it was worth the wait.

Long Island, N.Y., *Newsday*

Which story does that photo go with? It doesn't have a caption. Are these cruise ship passengers who got over their fright? Or is that the West Babylon woman and the pervert she tracked?

■ ■ ■ ■

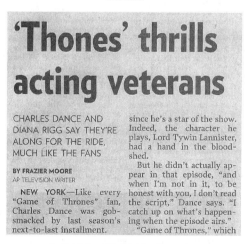

'Thones' thrills acting veterans

CHARLES DANCE AND DIANA RIGG SAY THEY'RE ALONG FOR THE RIDE, MUCH LIKE THE FANS

BY FRAZIER MOORE
AP TELEVISION WRITER

NEW YORK—Like every "Game of Thrones" fan, Charles Dance was gob-smacked by last season's next-to-last installment.

since he's a star of the show. Indeed, the character he plays, Lord Tywin Lannister, had a hand in the blood-shed.

But he didn't actually appear in that episode, "and when I'm not in it, to be honest with you, I don't read the script," Dance says. "I catch up on what's happening when the episode airs."

"Game of Thrones," which

Fredericksburg, Virginia, *Free Lance–Star*

In the thrilling Game of Thones, whoever can spell *Thrones* wins!

Appendix:
Questions and Answers

Questions From Writers

Q. How many periods go after a sentence?

A. Yes, I was really asked this. The answer: One is standard, though I often see two or none, and then I correct it.

Q. Sorry, I meant, how many spaces go after a sentence?

A. Two spaces after every sentence was standard for typewriting. For *typesetting*, one space is standard. (Look at any newspaper or any book by a major publisher.)

The *Franklin Covey Style Guide for Business and Technical Communication* says that one space is conventional for "current desktop publishing/word processing programs, which routinely use proportional spacing." This is different from what "many writers learned who gained their typing skills on typewriters, not personal computers." [216]

Q. If I'm referring to an institute in a formal letter; would I capitalize the *T* in "The Institute"?

A. No. *Words Into Type* says to capitalize *the* only if it's part of a name,[217] and such names are rare. The few examples it gives are all place names: The Dalles, Oregon; The Weirs, New Hampshire; The Hague, Netherlands. Two others are El Salvador and Los

Angeles. Although some organizations consider *The* to be part of their names (The George Washington University, for example), style guides generally reject capitalizing *The*. Similarly, I could call myself The Steve Dunham, but hardly anybody else would go along with it.

Q. Is *Internet* always capped? Or only when it refers to *the* Internet (as opposed to "internet capabilities")?

A. The *Computer Currents Interactive* dictionary said that *an* internet is "a network of networks; a group of networks interconnected via routers. The Internet (with a capital *I*) is the world's largest internet." *Technical Terms for Agribusiness Managers* says, "The Internet (short for internetworking, the practice of linking technologically different and independently operated networks), is a network of networks which allows users to communicate using electronic mail, to retrieve data stored in databases, and to access distant computers." Cap *Internet* if it refers to *the* Internet; "internet capabilities" probably refers to use of *the* Internet.[218]

Q. I'm interested in becoming a copy editor. What can you tell me?

A. Three useful (almost indispensable) books to me when I am editing are *Words Into Type*, *The Elements of Style*, and *The Associated Press Stylebook and Libel Manual*. Getting hold of them and studying them is a good start.

Words Into Type has two pages or so describing the work of a copy editor. Here is some of what it has to say.

> the copy editor is expected to read the text with care. He will make sure that proper names are spelled correctly, that dates are accurate, that quotations from Scripture and other classical works have been copied correctly....

> The copy editor must be familiar not only with the techniques of preparing manuscripts ... and with the conventions of book makeup ... but also with the details of

copy-editing style, typographical style, grammar, and the use of words.

Goodness knows I was not qualified in all that when I got my first editing job at Bell Labs more than thirty years ago. But I had a copy of *Words Into Type* and, even though I thought I knew more than I did, I was able to learn from others. And *Words Into Type* has most of the information that a copy editor should know.

The copy editor not only corrects writing but makes queries to the author and prepares the text for the layout person or printer. Nowadays most copy editing is done on computers rather than on paper, so it helps to be familiar with Microsoft Word or Word Perfect. Knowledge of HTML is a plus, too.

EEI in Alexandria, Virginia, has a three-day intensive introduction to copy editing. I used to teach the class. Having some EEI training is a plus when seeking editorial work. One thing EEI taught me is to use a checklist, because an editor simply cannot catch everything just by reading through a document. I just won't notice, for example, that some paragraphs have no punctuation at the end until I page through the document and look at only the ends of paragraphs.

So I highly recommend training and study. I hope this book helps a lot, too.

In an online chat, a reader posed a similar question (about becoming a copy editor) to *Washington Post* Assistant Managing Editor Don Podesta.

> **Columbia, Md.:** I recently obtained my BA in English Literature and would like to become a copy editor at a newspaper. What next?
>
> **Don Podesta:** Approach small- to medium-size local papers and ask whether there is a copy editing test you can take. If you worked for your college paper, a portfolio of clips would help. Most newspapers don't require entry-level editors to have degrees in journalism, but they

do require experience. If you have none yet, the best way to get in the door is to demonstrate that you have a knack and a passion for editing and can learn on the job quickly. But that would preclude most large metro dailies as a starting point.[219]

On her LibroEditing blog (libroediting.com), Liz Broomfield mentioned some qualifications for a career in proofreading or editing. Among other things, she said that you should:

- enjoy working on your own
- have a high attention span and a very high boredom threshold (I'm not saying that the work is boring: I love it; some people would be bored silly by it)
- write a very high standard of English[220]

Q. How do you find sources to verify names, titles, and quotations— especially if they contain errors?

A. Some reference sources, such as The Word Detective, The Quote Investigator (and more than fifty others), are in my Web favorites. Some I use every day. Others, such as a tree identification guide, I use less often, but I bookmarked them for the rare occasions when I do need them (such as when I was searching for a stock photo and found one marked "real pine" that the tree identification guide revealed to be probably a fir or spruce).

For books, I usually turn first to the Library of Congress online catalog. It's a very reliable resource, however not incapable of errors. One document I edited cited a book with "Systems Thing" in the title. To my astonishment, a search of the catalog turned up a book, but it was a mistake in the catalog. The entry said "Systems Thingking" when the real title was "Systems Thinking."

For almost everything else I start by copying the title, author surname, and some keywords from the quote into Notepad to get rid of any special characters that might interfere with a search and to pare down the search to essentials. For example,

I wouldn't include the author's first name in a Google search if I wasn't sure of the spelling. Sometimes searches take a long time, especially if there's an error in the author's name or the title: The searches might keep turning up nothing until I weed out the misspelled name. A one-page bibliography might take an hour or a whole afternoon to verify.

Especially with books in the public domain, I sometimes get lucky and find the whole thing on a university website or at Project Gutenberg (www.gutenberg.org) online. If I can't find an electronic copy of the book for free, I sometimes check public library catalogs, and on occasion, especially if there's a lot of material quoted, I borrow the book if it's available.

In the course of editing things, I save copies of documents I might need again.

Q. Oh sage,

When does one use "can not" versus "cannot"? (Is this one for the dumb question file?)

A. (I reproduced that question verbatim. The writer really did address me as "sage." The answer is verbatim, too.)

O, a single capital letter, is the "vocative O," vocative as in calling someone. "O Canada" is a well-known example. In the Canadian national anthem, the singer is calling or speaking to Canada. *Oh* is an interjection, something inserted into a sentence, as in "Oh, I see what you mean." Combined with a person's name in direct address, it should be set off by a comma. Calling a sage, use the vocative *O*: "O sage."

Cannot is standard. Separate words can be justified on occasion when it is important to emphasize *can* or *not*.

Q. When I describe the projects that I have completed in my current job, should I use past tense or current tense? Can I use both tenses in the current job description?

A. I don't think it matters as long as it's consistent, but personally I would use past tense to describe things I don't do anymore.

Q. Something about "Please RSVP to" doesn't sound right.

A. *RSVP* is French for "please reply." I would delete the *Please* in English or get rid of the French initials and just say *Please reply to.* Unless it actually says what it is supposed to say: Maybe at this point the hosts are begging invitees to reply.

Q. How do you reference a presentation in the bibliography?

A. Usually the point of a bibliography is to show the sources you used and to direct the reader to the sources for further reading. So if the presentation is available somewhere, that information should be included. Here is my idea of a hypothetical reference.

> Author's name, "Presentation title," presented at the ABCDE Conference, Aug. 9, 2005, Arlington, VA; available online at www.abcde.org/conferenceproceedings/author.html.

Q. Hypothetically, let's say I am making some pretty table tents [triangular cards with names printed on them] for some special visitors. I want to include their first and last names; however one of my guests is named "Steve Dunham IV." Does table-tent protocol dictate the inclusion of that "IV" on the table tent name? What about Steve Dunham Jr.? Technically Jr. is another way of saying Steve Dunham II.

A. (This question and answer are almost verbatim but slightly abbreviated.)

Mine should say, "The One, the Only, the Original Steve Dunham," although this is a slight exaggeration because there are impostors.

The Jr., Sr., I, II, III, etc., should be used if the people want them or if it's necessary to distinguish them from other family members. (That's why they're called "distinguished guests.") But

"II" is not the same as "junior": It indicates someone with the same name as a relative but not the same name as the parent.

Questions From a Technical Editing Class*

Q. What do contracting companies do, and where and how do they get their work?

> **A.** I've worked for only one government contractor, so I don't know a lot about what other companies may do. The company I worked for was created to do specific work, so it was sort of handed to the company at the beginning. Otherwise work is generally obtained through proposals—solicited or unsolicited—that lead to contracts.

Q. What types of projects do you work on and what purposes do they serve?

> **A.** In technical editing, I've gotten reports that go to the public, such as the unclassified version of the report of the USS *Cole* Commission; reports for clients, such as a quarterly technical report that was produced for the Ballistic Missile Defense Organization before it was morphed into the Missile Defense Agency; and documents for publication, such as articles for the *Journal of Homeland Security*. Reports that go to the public enable the government to communicate with the public; reports for clients document the work of company researchers; documents for publication provide a forum for discussion among professionals and the public.

Q. What skills did you need when you started, and what additional skills are necessary now?

> **A.** When I went to work at Bell Laboratories in 1981, editors didn't have computers, and the graphics were created by hand in an art studio or on big Genigraphics consoles. I had a pretty good

---

*   I didn't teach the class; I just answered some questions at the request of the instructor.

knowledge of English, some writing ability, and something of an eye for graphic composition. I had to acquire a basic knowledge of Bell Labs and what it was all about, and I learned editing as I went along.

Now knowledge of Microsoft Word or of WordPerfect is generally required. Knowledge of PowerPoint helps a lot, too, for editing on screen. Familiarity with the Internet is important, and a familiarity with library research helps, as well. I've done a lot of layout work, though mostly for publications that aren't technical. I've used PageMaker, QuarkXPress, InDesign, and plain-text HTML.

Q. What skills do you need that can't be taught in a classroom?

A. I think that writers and editors tend to have an innate aptitude for handling the language. My wife and I are both writers, and all our kids seem to have a creative spark and a literary streak. If somebody doesn't have an aptitude for English, I don't know whether it can be instilled. Attention to details, accuracy, and quality is a must, and I don't know whether it's possible to do a good job in this area if you don't first *care* about details, accuracy, and quality. Also, I'm not sure it *can't* be taught, but no class taught me how to communicate tactfully with authors. I'm still learning that.

Q. What additional responsibilities are involved in working with classified material?

A. Mainly it must be guarded and labeled. The requirements for labeling are quite detailed—how pages, paragraphs, and whole documents must be marked.

Q. Are clearances necessary for most contracting jobs, and what's involved in getting one?

A. If the client is the Defense Department, then some of the work will probably be classified. To handle that work, the editor needs the appropriate clearance even if the classified assignments make up a small part of the workload. Getting one is relatively simple: Your employer certifies that you need the clearance to do the work, and you fill out an electronic application that covers mainly the past seven years of your life.

Q. How much control do you have in the planning phase of a deliverable, and how much negotiation, if any, is involved in setting deadlines?

A. A few clients actually take the trouble to find out how much time and work are involved before bringing in work. Many do not, and sometimes we end up doing work of low quality because not enough time was allowed in the schedule for us to do a proper job.

Q. Whom do you work with most closely in your job—engineers, IT people, graphic designers, etc.?

A. I work most closely with graphic designers because we're all in the same room and we help each other out, but in terms of the editing itself, I work especially with the authors, who typically are analysts, though some are engineers or computer people. I also work a lot with editors of other publications, copy editing material they produce.

Q. When you need to hire a tech editor, how do you find one?

A. I and a part-time editor who worked here were hired under a temporary-to-permanent arrangement through agencies. We had one part-time editor who worked with me at a previous job. When the company needed another editor, I called to see whether she was interested; she interviewed and got the job. The company hires editors so infrequently that it's hard to say what the standard process would be.

Q. Do you use freelancers?

A. We occasionally use temps; I think the paperwork is what keeps us from using freelancers.

Q. What specs, military standards, or style guides do you use?

A. My main resource is *Words Into Type*, for three reasons: because it's so good, because I've been using it since 1975, and because the company had one or two copies on the shelf. The Chicago guide has too many rules for my taste and emphasizes academic publishing. My employer depended on the Government Printing Office manual for a long while, but it is more of a type-setting guide than a style guide and "is intended to facilitate Government printing." It is useful, though. So is the Associated Press guide, particularly for editing press releases.

Q. How do national and international events impact your workload or deliverables?

A. The attack on the USS *Cole* resulted in a commission that produced a classified report. The accident involving the Space Shuttle *Columbia* also resulted in a commission report. The lapse in airline security so forcefully demonstrated on September 11, 2001, resulted in many calls to the company because one division had been creating facial-recognition software for law enforcement, sponsored by the National Institute of Justice. Suddenly a lot of airports and other places saw the potential. The company got a lot of calls, resulting in press releases and op-ed pieces to edit. Also, company analysts used to cover Congressional hearings and write up reports, which we edited, often on short notice.

Q. What is a typical day like for you?

A. Often I will have one or more projects to work on, and I manage the workflow so as to get everything done on time. Journal articles may require only a couple of hours' work. Longer reports may take days or, rarely, weeks, especially if there are graphics for us to edit. On a typical day we will get a surprise job, sometimes with a conveniently loose schedule, sometimes with an impossibly short one, usually somewhere in between. The artists will normally have me check the small jobs, such as brochures and posters. Sometimes I am asked to write articles or to take photos.

Q. What do you enjoy most about your job?

> **A.** The people in the media group are great. We have a lot of fun working together. I've been with my current employer for seventeen years; all but one of my colleagues have been there longer. Sometimes I get to do work in which I have a free hand to make it as good as possible—I can clean up the writing, lay it out nicely, create something I'm satisfied with.

Q. What's the most challenging?

> **A.** Assignments that are on such a tight schedule that we can't do a proper job. Fortunately a lot of the people who bring us work appreciate what we can do and know that it takes time and effort. When they tell us to do it right and give us a free hand, that's satisfying.

Oh, How We Trip Over Our Own English Language

Laura Moyer's Red Pen column, Fredericksburg, Va., Free Lance–Star, *May 14, 2012. Reproduced with permission.*

I get funny emails from Red Pen reader and fellow editor Steve Dunham.

He spots gaffes that slip by *Free Lance–Star* editors. Here are some of our mistakes that Dunham has pointed out:

A headline about tsunamis was atop a story about typhoons. A Dr. Donahue headline referred to "profused bleeding." We mentioned a golfer from "Austrailia." We referred to people "of African decent."

We misused the word "dilemma" (it's a choice between unpleasant options, not just a bland quandary). We placed a story about the Oklahoma statehouse under a "Region" header. (Well, Oklahoma is in a region. Just not ours.)

In February we ran a Titanic-related headline: "A century later, tragedy at sea is popular."

Dunham wrote, "I knew people would like it if they just tried it."

Thank goodness not all his emails are about our mistakes.

In a recent email, he mentioned an ad in a [Virginia Railway Express] "Commuter Update" with the all-caps headline, "COMMUTERS DON'T HAVE TIME FOR INCOMPETANCE!"

The ad, for a heating company, went on to refer to a heating and cooling "diagnosis dictionary."

"I wish they would use the regular kind too," Dunham wrote.

Then there was the time the Arlington *Catholic Herald*, usually well-edited, published an item mentioning New York City's five "burrows."

"That's wrong," Dunham wrote. "New York has way more than five tunnels."

(It does, of course, have only five boroughs.)

In his professional life, Dunham has spotted some doozies.

Several years ago he was assigned to make an accurate transcript from a closed-captioned video of some hearings dealing with space. Among the phrases he discovered on the closed captions: "silly carbon" (Dunham imagined that to be a substance like Silly Putty, only black); "the photo register I watched them post" (the *Federal Register* and *The Washington Post*); and "using a rowboat for near-Earth missions." Turns out that was a robot.

More recently, he writes, "I was editing a book with a lot of medical content, and I came across 'in cases where all upper right to me is required.' I figured it was a phonetic misrepresentation of some medical term but I couldn't guess what."

He puzzled over it and finally asked the author, a doctor, what was meant.

It was "in cases where a laparotomy is required."

Dunham figured the doc must have dictated, and something got lost in transcription.

Because I didn't want to embarrass Dunham, I checked with him to make sure it was OK to use his name and examples in this column.

He responded that it was all upper right with him.

Check out Dunham's website, Steve Dunham's Trains of Thought, at www.stevedunham.50megs.com.

It has examples of his photography and humor writing, links to his published articles, and lessons about editing. Also, he really likes trains.

Notes

1. Laura Moyer, "Cellphone Camera at the Grocery Store," Red Pen blog, Fredericksburg, Va., *Free Lance–Star*, May 13, 2011.
2. Laura Moyer, "We Keep Trying," Red Pen blog, Fredericksburg, Va., *Free Lance–Star*, Nov. 29, 2011.
3. Arthur Plotnik, *The Elements of Editing: A Modern Guide for Editors and Journalists* (New York: Macmillan, 1982), p. xiii.
4. Arthur Plotnik, *The Elements of Editing*, p. 39.
5. *Merriam-Webster's Collegiate Dictionary*, 10th edition (Springfield, Mass.: Merriam-Webster, 1999).
6. Rich Adin, "On Language: The Professional Editor and the Hyphen," An American Editor blog, Oct. 1, 2012.
7. John E. McIntyre, "Count the Peeves," You Don't Say blog, *Baltimore Sun*, April 4, 2014.
8. Matt Young, *The Technical Writer's Handbook* (University Science Books, 1989).
9. Richard Mitchell, *Less Than Words Can Say* (Boston: Little, Brown, 1979).
10. Rich Adin, "The Business of Editing: Killing Me Softly," An American Editor blog, July 25, 2012.
11. John McIntyre, "Gag Me With a Copy Editor," You Don't Say blog, *Baltimore Sun*, Jan. 9, 2012.
12. Rufus Griscom, "The Fate of the Purple Spotted Editor: Evolve or Die," Moments in Succession blog, Nov. 18, 2010.
13. Rufus Griscom, "The Fate of the Purple Spotted Editor: Evolve or Die," comments.

14. "Why You Need to Proofread," Writing for the Web, *The Yahoo! Style Guide: Writing and Editing for the Web* (New York: St. Martin's Press, 2010).

15. "Why You Need to Proofread," Writing for the Web, *The Yahoo! Style Guide.*

16. Rufus Griscom, "The Fate of the Purple Spotted Editor: Evolve or Die."

17. Quoted in Rufus Griscom, "The Fate of the Purple Spotted Editor: Evolve or Die," comments.

18. Laura Moyer, "I'm a Prescriptivist, and I'm Proud," Red Pen blog, Fredericksburg, Va., *Free Lance-Star*, May 24, 2011.

19. William Safire, *The Language Maven Strikes Again* (New York: Doubleday, 1990), p. xiv.

20. George Orwell, "Politics and the English Language," *Horizon*, April 1946.

21. *Words Into Type*, 3rd Edition (Englewood Cliffs, NJ: Prentice-Hall, 1974), p. 57.

22. George Orwell, "Politics and the English Language."

23. Portions of this section appeared in *Precision for Writers and Editors*, September 1999; "Writing for Everybody," *Precision for Writers and Editors*, spring 2001; "Better Writing: Stating the Obvious," *Transmissions*, June–July 2001; and "Big Thinks" and "Word Abuse," *Precision for Writers and Editors*, Autumn 2001; all copyright Analytic Services Inc. and are used with permission.

24. William Lutz, *Doublespeak* (New York: Harper & Row, 1989).

25. William Safire, *In Love with Norma Loquendi* (New York: Random House, 1994).

26. William Safire, *Spread the Word* (New York: Times Books, 1999).

27. Edwin Newman, *A Civil Tongue* (New York: Warner Books, 1976).

28. Portions of this section appeared in *Precision for Writers and Editors*, September 1999, copyright Analytic Services Inc., and are used with permission.

29. George Orwell, "Politics and the English Language."

30. Fred L. Schultz, "Interview: Stephen Coonts," U.S. Naval Institute *Proceedings*, vol. 127, no. 7, July 2001, p. 68.

31. Laura Moyer, "Rock. Copy Editor. Hard Place," Red Pen blog, Fredericksburg, Va., *Free Lance–Star*, June 7, 2011.

32. Laura Moyer, "Lie/Lay. I Had to Tackle This Sometime," Red Pen blog, Fredericksburg, Va., *Free Lance–Star*, Aug. 2, 2011.

33. William M. Fowler, Jr., *Under Two Flags: The American Navy in the Civil War* (New York: W. W. Norton, 1990).

34. Arthur Plotnik, *The Elements of Editing*, p. 3.

35. Arthur Plotnik, *The Elements of Editing*, pp. 35–36.

36. Rufus Griscom, "The Fate of the Purple Spotted Editor: Evolve or Die."

37. Fred L. Schultz, "Interview: Stephen Coonts."

38. Candi Harrison, "I've Said It Before and I'll Say It Again ... 5 Principles of Customer Service," Candi On Content blog, Feb. 22, 2012.

39. *Words Into Type*, p. 57.

40. Rufus Griscom, "The Fate of the Purple Spotted Editor: Evolve or Die."

41. Arthur Plotnik, *The Elements of Editing*, p. 26.

42. *The Associated Press Stylebook and Libel Manual* (New York: Associated Press, 1997), p. 147.

43. Robert D. Smith, *The Other Side of Christ* (Avon, NJ: Magnificat Press, 1987), pp. 15–16.

44. Judith Martin, *Miss Manners Rescues Civilization* (New York: Crown Publishers, 1996), p. 368.

45. Plain Language Action Network, *Writing User-Friendly Documents* (now called the Plain Language Action and Information Network and *Writing Reader-Friendly Documents*).

46. Richard Mitchell, *Less Than Words Can Say*.

47. Michael Quinion, "Meeting Room Jargon," World Wide Words blog, Feb. 26, 2000.

48. "Translate Voice Into Words," Writing for the Web, *The Yahoo! Style Guide*.

49. "Write for an International Audience," Writing for the Web, *The Yahoo! Style Guide.*

50. Candi Harrison, "Web Management 101," Candi On Content blog, March 28, 2012.

51. Candi Harrison, "The Answer for Better Searching? Better Content!" Candi On Content blog, Dec. 12, 2007.

52. Paul G. Hayes, "The Novel Art of Verbing," *Trains*, January 1991, reprinted from *Wisconsin*, the Sunday magazine of the Milwaukee *Journal*, Jan. 8, 1989.

53. Some of the following material appeared as "Put Jargon in Its Place" in *Precision for Writers and Editors*, spring 2000, copyright Analytic Services Inc., and is used with permission.

54. Richard Mitchell, *Less Than Words Can Say.*

55. John Holdren, "What Are We Thinking? What Are We Saying?" *Common Knowledge*, volume 8, no. 4, fall 1995.

56. John Holdren, "What Are We Thinking? What Are We Saying?"

57. Richard Mitchell, *Less Than Words Can Say.*

58. John Holdren, "What Are We Thinking? What Are We Saying?"

59. Richard Mitchell, *Less Than Words Can Say.*

60. Printed dictionaries, published infrequently, cannot keep up with usage. An excellent online source is OneLook Dictionaries (www.onelook.com), which searches many dictionaries (including specialized ones) at once.

61. Michael Quinion, "Collins English Dictionary," World Wide Words blog, Nov. 6, 2010.

62. "Plain Language" appeared in *Precision for Writers and Editors*, September 1999, copyright Analytic Services Inc., and is used with permission.

63. Candi Harrison, "Plain Language Is Good Business," Candi On Content blog, Dec. 19, 2012.

64. Candi Harrison, "'Plain Language' Is More Than Words," Candi On Content blog, Nov. 5, 2012.

65. www.plainlanguage.gov.

66. George Orwell, "Politics and the English Language."

67. Barbara Tuchman, *The First Salute: A View of the American Revolution* (New York: Alfred A. Knopf, 1988).

68. Rufus Griscom, "The Fate of the Purple Spotted Editor: Evolve or Die."

69. Christopher T. Baer, William J. Coxey, and Paul W. Schopp, *The Trail of the Blue Comet* (Palmyra, NJ: West Jersey Chapter of the National Railway Historical Society, 1994).

70. Rev. James Groenings, SJ, *The Passion of Jesus and Its Hidden Meaning* (Rockford, IL: TAN; originally published St. Louis, Mo.: B. Herder, 1908).

71. James Steele, *Queen Mary* (London: Phaidon, 1995).

72. Michael A. Bailin, Foreword, in Tony Proscio, "In Other Words: A Plea for Plain Speaking in Foundations," Edna McConnell Clark Foundation, 2000.

73. Federal Emergency Management Agency, *Are You Ready? An In-depth Guide to Citizen Preparedness*, 2004.

74. Independent Panel to Review Department of Defense Detention Operations, August 2004.

75. Bruce Portzer, entry that won a "dishonorable mention" in the Bulwer-Lytton Fiction Contest, Nancy Bartley, "Local Writers Win Bad-Prose Prizes," *Seattle Times*, Aug. 7, 2008.

76. Miguel de Cervantes, *Don Quixote* (1615), translated by John Ormsby, vol. 2, chap. 64.

77. Brendan Gill, *Here at The New Yorker* (New York: Random House, 1975), p. 161.

78. William Safire, *Coming to Terms* (Garden City, NY: Doubleday, 1991).

79. John McIntyre, "First Day of [Editing] Class," You Don't Say blog, *Baltimore Sun*, Aug. 23, 2011.

80. Laura Moyer, "You Could Read It Another Way," Red Pen blog, Fredericksburg, Va., *Free Lance-Star*, Oct. 10, 2011.

81. U.S. Department of Justice, press release, May 4, 2004.

82. Rich Adin, "The Drama of 'And' and 'Or,'" An American Editor blog, March 11, 2013.

83. William Safire, *Let a Simile Be Your Umbrella* (New York: Crown Publishers, 2001), pp. 164–165.
84. www.word-detective.com.
85. Evan Morris, Word Detective, Sep. 3, 2004.
86. Evan Morris, Word Detective, Dec. 5, 2005.
87. William Safire, *Watching My Language* (New York: Random House, 1997).
88. "Talk to the Newsroom: Managing Editor John Geddes," online chat, *The New York Times* website, Jan. 14, 2008.
89. Richard Mitchell, *Less Than Words Can Say*.
90. Parts of "Careful Word Choice" appeared in *Precision for Writers and Editors*, spring 2000, copyright Analytic Services Inc., and are used with permission.
91. Laura Moyer, "Because, You Know, There Are So Many Good Ones," Red Pen blog, Fredericksburg, Va., *Free Lance–Star*, July 12, 2012.
92. *Writer's Handbook* , Writing Center, University of Wisconsin–Madison, 2014.
93. *Words Into Type*, p. 341.
94. *Words Into Type*, p. 341.
95. E.J. Dionne, Jr., "Under Observation: Chattering Class," *The Washington Post Magazine*, Feb. 23, 1997, p. 2.
96. William Safire, *Freedom*, "Underbook: Sources and Commentary" (Garden City, NY: Doubleday, 1987), p. 978.
97. Richard Corfield, *Lives of the Planets: A Natural History of the Solar System* (New York: Basic Books, 2007), p. 190.
98. "Check It Out," *Editor's Workshop*, October 1992, p. 12.
99. Jim Lehrer, *A Bus of My Own* (New York: G.P. Putnam's Sons, 1992), p. 125.
100. Ed Jones, "MGM's Errant Obit Is Lesson for Journalists," Fredericksburg, Va., *Free Lance–Star*, April 19, 2006.
101. Michael Gerson, "Journalism's Slow, Sad Death," *Washington Post*, Nov. 27, 2009.

102. Some of the following material appeared as "Accuracy Counts" in *Precision for Writers and Editors*, winter 2000, copyright Analytic Services Inc., and is used with permission.

103. "Point/Counterpoint—Can You Edit a Direct Quotation?" *The Editorial Eye*, July 1996, pp. 6–7.

104. *The Associated Press Stylebook and Libel Manual* (New York: Associated Press, 1997), p. 172.

105. Laura Moyer, "Misspoken? Or Misheard?" Red Pen blog, Fredericksburg, Va., *Free Lance–Star*, Aug. 23, 2011.

106. Laura Moyer, "Misspoken? Or Misheard?"

107. *Words Into Type*, p. 58.

108. Laura Moyer, "Just the Facts (Today's Red Pen Contest Answers)," Red Pen blog, Fredericksburg, Va., *Free Lance–Star*, July 9, 2012.

109. Motoko Rich, "Pondering Good Faith in Publishing," *The New York Times*, March 9, 2010.

110. Laura Moyer, "Inevitable," Red Pen blog, Fredericksburg, Va., *Free Lance–Star*, May 17, 2011.

111. Most of this section appeared as "Name That Exponent," in *Precision for Writers and Editors*, spring 2000, copyright Analytic Services Inc., and is used with permission.

112. www.mathleague.com.

113. Barbara De Lollis, "Internet Error Puts Starwood in No-Win Situation," *USA Today*, Jan. 14, 2003.

114. Helen Altonn, "Hot Dogs Raise Risk of Cancer, Study Says," *Honolulu Star-Bulletin*, April 21, 2005.

115. William Safire, *Let a Simile Be Your Umbrella*, p. 237.

116. Priscilla S. Taylor, "The Watchful Eye—A Cautionary Tale: Inadvertent Plagiarism," *The Editorial Eye*, September 1996, p. 7.

117. "The Flawed Report of the Heritage Foundation," editorial, *Manila Times* (Philippines), Jan. 11, 2006.

118. Stacy Schiff, "Know It All: Can Wikipedia Conquer Expertise?" *The New Yorker*, July 31, 2006.

119. Philip Roth, "An Open Letter to Wikipedia," *The New Yorker*, Sep. 7, 2012.

120. Stacy Schiff, "Know It All: Can Wikipedia Conquer Expertise?"

121. Evan Morris, Word Detective column on the word *wiki*, April 2009.

122. Maria Bustillos, "Wikipedia and the Death of the Expert," *The Awl*, May 17, 2011.

123. Maria Bustillos, "Wikipedia and the Death of the Expert."

124. Maria Bustillos, "Wikipedia and the Death of the Expert."

125. Ivars Peterson, "Flight of the Bumblebee," *Science News Online*, March 29, 1997.

126. www.HomeworkSpot.com.

127. Homework Spot, "Evaluating Resources: When Is a Site Trustworthy?"

128. Homework Spot, "Evaluating Resources."

129. Garson O'Toole, "You Don't Have to Know Everything. You Just Have to Know Where to Find It," Quote Investigator, April 2, 2012.

130. "Student's Wikipedia Hoax Dupes Journalists," Reuters, Toronto *Star*, May 7, 2009.

131. Maria Konnikova, "'Beam Us Up, Mr. Scott!': Why Misquotations Catch On," *Atlantic*, Aug. 15, 2012.

132. Garson O'Toole, "Compound Interest Is Man's Greatest Invention," Quote Investigator, Oct. 31, 2011.

133. William Safire, *On Language*.

134. "Beneficial Bibliographies" appeared in different form in *Precision for Writers and Editors*, winter 2001, copyright Analytic Services Inc., and is used with permission.

135. Evan Morris, Word Detective, undated.

136. William Safire, *The Language Maven Strikes Again*.

137. Mary Stoughton, "Infernal English—A Special Hell for the Fraudulent?" *The Editorial Eye*, August 1996.

138. Joann Byrd, "14 Hot Complaints."

139. David E. Fessenden, *Concept to Contract: Writing the Christian Nonfiction Book* (Galax, VA: Sonfire Media, 2011).
140. *Words Into Type*, p. 58.
141. Joann Byrd, "14 Hot Complaints."
142. *Words Into Type*, p. 362.
143. Laura Moyer, "That 's' Is Important," Red Pen blog, Fredericksburg, Va., *Free Lance-Star*, July 12, 2011.
144. Sam McManis, "Sportscasters Who Try a Grammarian's Soul," *San Francisco Chronicle*, March 26, 2002.
145. "His 'n' Her Pronouns" appeared in *Precision for Writers and Editors*, winter 2001, copyright Analytic Services Inc., and is used with permission.
146. Laura Moyer, "Where Men Are Men, and Women Are People," Red Pen blog, Fredericksburg, Va., *Free Lance-Star*, June 14, 2011.
147. Guidelines for Nonsexist Use of Language in NCTE Publications (Revised, 1985).
148. Evan Morris, "The Epicene Epic," Word Detective column, May 4, 1997.
149. Guidelines for Nonsexist Use of Language in NCTE Publications.
150. Guidelines for Nonsexist Use of Language in NCTE Publications.
151. "Mistaken Junction" appeared in *Transmissions*, autumn 2001, copyright Analytic Services Inc., and is reprinted with permission.
152. William Safire, *Take My Word for It* (New York: Times Books, 1986), pp. 73–75.
153. Portions of this section appeared in "Hyphens Are Our Friends," *Precision for Writers and Editors*, winter 2001, copyright Analytic Services Inc., and are used with permission.
154. This section appeared as "On, Dasher" in *Precision for Writers and Editors*, spring 2001, copyright Analytic Services Inc., and is used with permission.

155. "Parentheses and Brackets" appeared in slightly different form in *Precision for Writers and Editors*, summer 2001, and "Fragments on the Doorstep" appeared in the winter 2000 issue, both copyright Analytic Services Inc. and used with permission.

156. *Words Into Type*, p. 212.

157. This appeared as "Slash the Slash" in *Precision for Writers and Editors*, September 1999, copyright Analytic Services Inc., and is used with permission.

158. *Words Into Type*, p. 500.

159. Richard Mitchell, *The Graves of Academe* (New York: Simon & Schuster, 1987).

160. "Ellipsis Points" appeared in *Precision for Writers and Editors*, spring 2000, copyright Analytic Services Inc., and is used with permission.

161. *Words Into Type*, p. 20.

162. *Words Into Type*, p. 225.

163. *Words Into Type*, p. 225.

164. This section appeared in different form as "Colon and Semicolon" in *Precision for Writers and Editors*, autumn 2001, copyright Analytic Services Inc., and is used with permission.

165. William Safire, *Let a Simile Be Your Umbrella*, p. 271.

166. Carol Fisher Saller, *The Subversive Copy Editor* (University of Chicago Press, 2009).

167. Rich Adin, "What Do Editors Forget Most Often?" An American Editor blog, March 4, 2013.

168. *Words Into Type*, pp. 237–239.

169. Julie Wright, "Keeping Things Together," *Precision for Writers and Editors*, winter 2001, copyright Analytic Services Inc., used with permission.

170. Robin Williams, *The Non-Designer's Design Book*, 3rd edition (Berkeley, Cal.: Peachpit Press, 2008).

171. Robin Williams, *The Non-Designer's Type Book* (Berkeley, Cal.: Peachpit Press, 1998).

172. Robin Williams and John Tollett, *The Non-Designer's Web Book*, 3rd edition (Berkeley, Cal.: Peachpit Press, 2005).

173. Rich Adin, An American Editor blog, "When Editors and Authors Fail," March 6, 2013.

174. Laura Moyer, "Always Wrong," Red Pen blog, Fredericksburg, Va., *Free Lance-Star*, May 11, 2011.

175. Laura Moyer, "Always Wrong."

176. "Strange Traditions" appeared in *Precision for Writers and Editors*, summer 2001, copyright Analytic Services Inc., and is used with permission.

177. William Safire, *Take My Word for It* (New York: Times Books, 1986).

178. William Safire, *Take My Word for It* (New York: Times Books, 1986).

179. This section appeared as "The Country Formerly Known as ..." in *Precision for Writers and Editors*, winter 2000, copyright Analytic Services Inc., and is used with permission.

180. Tom Clancy, *SSN* (New York: Berkley Books, 1996).

181. Portions of "Homophones and Other Words That Get Mixed Up" appeared in slightly different form in "But I Ran a Spellcheck" in ANSER *Transmissions*, March–April 1999, and in "On Screen: Bad Words," *Precision for Writers and Editors*, spring 2001, both copyright Analytic Services Inc., and are used with permission.

182. "Acronym Soup" appeared in slightly different form in ANSER *Transmissions*, May–June 1999.

183. William Safire, *Watching My Language*.

184. www.plainlanguage.gov.

185. Part of this section previously appeared as "Chicken-or-Egg Capitalization" in *Precision for Writers and Editors*, spring 2001, copyright Analytic Services Inc., and is used with permission.

186. William Safire, *No Uncertain Terms* (New York: Simon & Schuster, 2004).

187. "Initially Redundant" appeared in *Precision for Writers and Editors*, September 1999, copyright Analytic Services Inc., and is used with permission.

188. "Steps to Better Writing" was created in 1998 as a presentation for a technical writing class at Analytic Services Inc., and portions of it are used here with permission.

189. Laura Moyer, "Feeling Impolite," Red Pen blog, Fredericksburg, Va., *Free Lance-Star*, Feb. 8, 2012.

190. *Merriam-Webster's Collegiate Dictionary*, 10th edition.

191. Ambrose Bierce, *The Devil's Dictionary*, 1911.

192. John McIntyre, "Colossal! Epic! Glorious!" You Don't Say blog, *Baltimore Sun*, Oct. 28, 2011.

193. "Clear Out Deadwood," Writing for the Web, *The Yahoo! Style Guide*.

194. Gloria Cooper, *Red Tape Holds Up New Bridge* (New York: Perigee, 1987); *Squad Helps Dog Bite Victim* (New York: Doubleday, 1980).

195. *Words Into Type*, p. 60.

196. Liz Broomfield, "On Being Edited," LibroEditing blog, Feb. 13, 2013.

197. Evan Morris, the Word Detective, "My Back Pages," July 23, 2002.

198. Richard Mitchell, *Less Than Words Can Say*.

199. "Other Uses of the Spell-Checker" appeared in *Precision for Writers and Editors*, autumn 1999, copyright Analytic Services Inc., and is used with permission.

200. *Words Into Type*, p. 135.

201. "Editing on Paper or On-Screen?" appeared in slightly different form in "But I Ran a Spellcheck" in ANSER *Transmissions*, March–April 1999, copyright Analytic Services Inc., and is used with permission.

202. Most of the section "Editorial Tasks" appeared in slightly different form in "But I Ran a Spellcheck" in ANSER *Transmissions*, March–April 1999, copyright Analytic Services Inc., and is used

with permission. Some of it appeared in *Precision for Writers and Editors*, September 1999, copyright Analytic Services Inc., and likewise is used with permission.

203. Laura Moyer, "The Commas and the Damage Done," Red Pen blog, Fredericksburg, Va., *Free Lance–Star*, Aug. 9, 2011.
204. Laura Moyer, "The Commas and the Damage Done."
205. Jean Hollis Weber, "The Role of the Editor in the Technical Writing Team," Proceedings of the Technical Communication Seminar, 1990.
206. "How Long Does Editing Take?" appeared in slightly different form in "But I Ran a Spellcheck," ANSER *Transmissions*, March–April 1999, copyright Analytic Services Inc., and is used with permission.
207. "Cheap, Quick Quality?" appeared in *Precision for Writers and Editors*, summer 2001, copyright Analytic Services Inc., and is used with permission.
208. Anne Applebaum, *Iron Curtain: The Crushing of Eastern Europe, 1944-1956* (New York: Doubleday, 2012), p. 383.
209. *Words Into Type*, p. 58.
210. David S. Broder, *Behind the Front Page* (New York: Touchstone, 1987).
211. Laura Moyer, "In the Soup," Red Pen blog, Fredericksburg, Va., *Free Lance–Star*, May 4, 2011.
212. This appeared in slightly different form as "The AP Stylebook—Not Just for Journalists" in *Precision for Writers and Editors*, winter 2000, copyright Analytic Services Inc., and is used with permission.
213. Richard Mitchell, *Less Than Words Can Say*.
214. John McIntyre, "Tout," You Don't Say blog, *Baltimore Sun*, January 20, 2014.
215. *Words Into Type*, p. 20.
216. *Franklin Covey Style Guide for Business and Technical Communication* (Salt Lake City, Utah: Franklin Covey Co., 1997), p. 291.

217. *Words Into Type*, p. 169.

218. This question and answer are from *Precision for Writers and Editors*, spring 2000, copyright Analytic Services Inc., reproduced with permission.

219. "Ask the Post," online chat with *Washington Post* Assistant Managing Editor Don Podesta, May 3, 2006.

220. Liz Broomfield, "Proofreading as a Career—Some Pointers," LibroEditing blog, October 26, 2011.

Index

unorthodox, 106
Puns, unintentional, 128
Purdue Online Writing Lab, The, 155
Pyramid, inverted, 12, 37, 45
Quinion, Michael, 28, 32
Quote Investigator, The, 75–76, 155
Quotes, 59–65
    altering, 60–61
    attributing, 70–71, 76–77, 178
    editing, 60–61
    errors in, 60–61, 63–65, 76–78, 203
    excerpted, 165
    formatting, 60–62
    indenting, 60, 62
    punctuating, 60, 62, 162–163
    repeated, 150–151
    secondhand, 75–77
    styling, 63
    transcribing, 60–61, 77
    verifying, 63–64, 77, 139, 147, 165–166, 203–204
Readers
    editing for, 22–38
    expert, 71
    foreign, 28
    knowing the, 24–27
    working with, 134–135
    writing for, 2, 11, 22–27
Research, 55–56, 155
Resources, print and online, 152–156
Safire, William, 8, 77, 79–80, 123
    Janus words, 49, 160
    on punctuation, 96, 106
    on word use, 15–16, 47, 51, 116–117
Sentences, parts of, 89–94
    fragments, 6, 89, 101
    mistaken junction, 91–92
    nonrestrictive clause, 93, 95, 115–116
    restrictive clause, 95, 115–116
    series, 96
    subjects, predicates and objects, 34, 90
    See also Words

Sources, 58–59, 63, 72, 77
    attributing, 56, 70–71, 78, 80, 205
    finding, 203–205
    reliability of, 71–75
    Internet, 74–75
Spell-checking, 117–119, 139–142, 162, 177, 185
Style guides, 106–108, 209
    See also under specific guide
Style sheets, 137
Tables, 21, 24, 186
Technical editing, 136, 146, 206–210
    See also Terms, technical
Technical Editors' Eyrie, The, 146, 155
Technical writing, 34, 40, 45, 102
Terms, 29, 152–153
    Latin, 60
    shorthand, 121
    technical, 9, 28, 30, 40, 155
Text
    hidden, 140
    jumps, 139
    justified, 139
Titles, 138, 161, 166–167, 203–204
    type styling of, 63
Tone, 25, 34, 40, 42, 87
    purposes of, 51–52
Transcripts, 60–61, 77, 212
Trim, page, 140
Typesetting, 112, 200
Typography, 109–113
    checking, 138–139
    line breaks, 109–111
    superscript, 139, 141
    text boxes, 113, 186
    word breaks, 109
Typos, 1, 20, 162, 169, 179, 188, 193, 199
Underground Grammarian, The, 4, 52, 135, 155–156
Voice, 34, 54–56
Walsh, Bill, 60
Weber, Jean Hollis, 146